SMOOTH STONES

TAKEN

FROM ANCIENT BROOKS

by

Rev. C.H. Spurgeon

being a collection of sentences, illustrations,
and quaint sayings, from the works of that
renowned Puritan, Thomas Brooks

Soli Deo Gloria Publications
...for instruction in righteousness...

Soli Deo Gloria Publications

P.O. Box 451, Morgan, PA 15064
(412) 221-1901/FAX 221-1902

*

Smooth Stones Taken from Ancient Brooks
was first published in 1860 by Sheldon
& Company in New York. This
Soli Deo Gloria reprint is 1996.
Printed in the USA.

*

ISBN 1-57358-027-9

PREFACE.

As a writer, Brooks scatters stars with both his hands: he hath dust of gold; in his storehouse are all manner of precious stones. Genius is always marvelous; but when sanctified it is matchless. The ringing of the bells of the sanctuary is sweeter than the music of the house of feasting. Had Brooks been a worldly man, his writings would have been most valuable; but since he was an eminent Christian, they are doubly so. He had the eagle eye of faith, as well as the eagle wing of imagination. He saw similes, metaphors, and allegories everywhere; but they were all consecrated to his Master's service: his heart indited the good matter, for he spake of the things which he had made touching the King.

Reader, thou hast here presented to thee, in a cheap and readable form, the choice sayings of one of the King's mighties. The great divine who wrote these precious sentences was of the race of the giants. He was head and shoulders above all the people, not in his stature (like Saul), but in mind, and soul, and grace. Treasure these gems, and adorn thyself with them, by putting them into the golden setting of holy practice, which is the end the writer always aimed at. Use these "smooth stones" as David of old, and may the Lord direct them to the very forehead of thy sins, for this is the author's main design!

One of these pithy extracts may assist our meditations for a whole day, and may open up some sweet passage of Scripture to our understandings, and perhaps some brief sentence may stick in the sinner's conscience, like an arrow from the bow of God.

So prays the servant of Christ and His Church,

C. H. SPURGEON.

MEMOIR.

Mr. Thomas Brooks was a very affecting preacher, and useful to many. Though he used many homely phrases, and sometimes too familiar resemblances, which to nice critics might appear ridiculous, he did more good to souls than many who deliver the most exact compositions. And let the wits of the age pass what censures they please, "he that winneth souls is wise." Mr. Brooks had been for some time preacher at St. Thomas Apostle, and about the year 1651 was chosen by the majority of the parishioners of St. Mary Magdalen. Gathering a church there in the congregational way, the rest of the parish preferred a petition against him to the committee of ministers, and he published a defense against their charges. He died September 27th, 1680. His friend, Mr. Reeve, preached his funeral sermon and succeeded him.*

Mr. Baxter makes especial mention of Mr. Brooks,

* In some of his works he writes himself, "Late preacher of the word of St. Margaret's, New Fish Street." See his "Mute Christian."

1*

amongst those independent ministers who opened their meetings more publicly than before, after the fire of London. His farewell address to his people (which has no text) appears to have been published by himself. It is peculiarly adapted for usefulness. We shall therefore here introduce a full analysis of it, and the rather, as the account of Mr. Brooks is so brief. It will give the reader a more just idea of the man than any thing that could be said of him. He first answers three queries, viz., 1. Why men make such opposition to the plain, powerful, consci- entious preaching of the gospel? 2. What goes from a people when the gospel goes? Answer: Peace, prosperity, safety, civil liberty, true glory, and soul-happiness, the presence of God. (2 Chron- icles, xiii. 9; xv. 3, 5, 6; 1 Samuel, iv. 22; Jere- miah, ii. 11–13.) 3. Whether God will remove the gospel from England? Many reasons to hope the contrary. There may be a darkness upon it, but when it is darkest it is nearest day.

He then proceeds to give his people some hints of advice, which he calls legacies, hoping they might be of use to them in the perusal when he had not the advantage of speaking to them in public. 1. Se- cure your interest in Christ. This is not a time for a man to be between *hopes and fears*. Take not up with an outward form, crying, "The Temple of

the Lord." 2. Make Christ and Scripture the only
foundation for your souls, and for faith to build
upon. 3. In all places and companies, be sure to
carry your soul-preservatives with you, (a holy care
and wisdom), as men carry outward preservatives
with them in infectious times. 4. See that all your
graces, your faith, love, courage, zeal, resolution,
magnanimity, rise higher by opposition, threaten-
ings, and sufferings. Say as David, if this be vile, I
will be more vile. 5. Take more pains to keep
yourselves from sin than from suffering. (Acts, ii.
40; Revelations, iii. 4.) 6. Be always doing or receiving good. This will make your lives comfortable, your deaths happy, and your account glorious
in the great day of the Lord. 7. Set the highest
examples of grace and godliness before you for im-
itation. Next to that of Christ, the pattern of the
choicest saints. For faith, Abraham; for courage,
Joshua; for uprightness, Job; for meekness, Moses,
&c. 8. Hold fast your integrity. Let all go rather
than let that go. (Job, xxvii. 5, 6.) 9. Let not a
day pass without calling the whole man to an exact
account. Hands.—What have you done for God to
day? Tongue.—What have you spoke? &c. 10.
Labor for a healing spirit. Away with all discrim-
inating names that may hinder the applying of balm
to heal our wounds. Discord and division become

no Christian. For wolves to worry the lambs is no wonder, but for one lamb to worry another is unnatural and monstrous. 11. Be most in the spiritual exercises of religion, meditation, self-examination, &c. Bodily exercises without these will profit nothing. 12. Take no truths upon trust, but all upon trial. Bring all to the balance of the sanctuary. (1 Thessalonians, v. 21; Acts, xvii. 11.) It was the glory of that church that they would not trust Paul himself. 13. The fewer opportunities and the lesser advantages you have in public, the more abundantly address yourselves to God in private. (Malachi, iii. 16, 17.) 14. Walk in those ways that are directly contrary to the vain, sinful, superstitious ways that men of a formal, carnal, lukewarm spirit walk in. 15. Look upon all the things of this world as you will when you come to die. Men may now put a mask upon them, but then they will appear in their own colors. 16. Never put off conscience with any plea that you dare not stand by in the great day of your account. 17. Eye more the internal workings of God in your souls, than the external providences of God. If God should carry on ever so glorious a work in the world as the conquest of nations to Christ, what would it advantage thee if sin, Satan, and the world triumph in thy soul? 18. Look as well on the bright as well as on the

dark side of Providence. 19. Keep up precious
thoughts of God, under his sharpest and severest
dispensations to you. 20. Hold on and hold out in
the ways of well-doing in the want of all outward
discouragements. (Revelations, ii. 10.) Follow ye
the Lamb, though others follow the beast and the
false prophet. 21. In all your natural, civil, and
religious actions, let divine glory rest upon your
souls; let the glory of Christ lie nearest your hearts.
22. Record all special favors, mercies, providences,
and experiences. Little do you know the advantages that will redound to your souls upon this.
23. Never enter upon the trial of your (spiritual)
estate, but when your hearts are in the fittest temper. 24. Always make the Scripture, and not your
carnal reason, or your bare opinion (or that of others) the rule by which to judge of your spiritual
condition. (Isaiah, viii. 20; John, xii. 48.) 25.
Make conscience of making good the terms on
which you closed with Christ, viz., that you would
deny yourselves, take up the cross, &c. 26. Walk
by no rule but such as you dare die by, and stand
by in the day of Jesus Christ. Walk not with the
multitude. Make not the example of great men
your rule, that stands in opposition to Jesus Christ.
Who dare stand by either of these before him at
the great day? 27. Lastly. Sit down and rejoice

with fear. Rejoice in what God hath done for your
souls by the everlasting gospel. Weep that you
have done no more to improve it, and that you
have so neglected the opportunities of enriching
your souls. Here are your legacies. The Lord
make them of singular use to you, that you may
give up your account to the great and glorious God
with joy. Make conscience of putting these things
into practice till you shall be brought to the fruition
of God, where you shall need ordinances, preaching,
and praying no more.

SMOOTH STONES

TAKEN

FROM ANCIENT BROOKS.

CHRIST often takes the crown off his own head, and puts it upon the head of faith; witness such passages as these, which are frequent in Scripture: "Thy faith hath saved thee," (Luke, vii. 50). "Thy faith hath made thee whole," (Matthew, ix. 22). And no wonder that Christ crowns faith, for of all graces, faith takes the crown off a man's own head, and puts it upon the head of Christ.

The little word "father," (said Luther,) lisped forth in prayer by a child of God, exceeds the eloquence of Demosthenes, Cicero, and all the other famed orators of the world.

Sin is bad in the eye, worse in the tongue, worse still in the heart, but worst of all in the life.

It was a good saying of one to a great lord, upon his showing his stately house, and pleasant gardens: "Sir, you had need make sure of heaven, or else, when you die, you will be a very great loser."

If you would be good betimes, you must acquaint yourselves with *yourselves* betimes. No man begins to be good till he sees himself to be bad. The ready way to be found is to see ourselves lost. The first step to mercy, is to see our own misery; the first step toward heaven, is to see ourselves near hell.

Ah, believer, it is only heaven that is above all winds, storms, and tempests; God did not cast man out of paradise, that he might be able to find himself another paradise in this world. The world and you must part, or Christ and you will never meet. " Ye can not serve God and mammon."

"Speak, that I may see thee," said Socrates to a fair boy. We know metals by their tinkling, and men by their talking. Happy was that tongue in the primitive time, that could sound out any thing of David's doing; but how much happier is he who can tell any thing of Christ from sweet experience!

"Let the thoughts of a crucified Christ," said one, "be never out of your mind. Let them be meat and drink unto you. Let them be your sweetness and consolation, your honey and your desire, your reading and your meditation, your life, death, and resurrection."

There is no time yours but the present time, no day yours but the present day; therefore, do not please and feed yourselves with hopes of time to come ; that you will repent, but not yet; and lay hold on mercy, but not yet; and give yourselves up to the Lord next week, next month, or next year; for that God who has promised you mercy and favor upon the day of your return, has not promised to prolong your lives till that day comes.

O how strong is grace! How victorious over sin, how dead to the world, how alive to Christ, how fit to live, and how prepared to die, might many a Christian have become had they been

2

more frequent, serious, and conscientious in the discharge of closet duties!

It is the very nature of grace to make a man strive to be most eminent in that particular grace which is most opposed to his bosom sin.

Young men are very apt to compare them-selves with those who are worse than they are, and this proves a snare unto them, and often-times their ruin, as it did to the Pharisee in the gospel, who pleaded his negative righteousness; he was not as other men are, extortioners, unjust, adulterers, nor even as the publican; he stood not only upon his comparisons, but upon his dis-parisons: being blind at home, and too quick-sighted abroad, he contemns the poor publican who was better than himself, making good that saying of Seneca, "The nature of man is very apt to use spectacles to behold other men's faults, rather than looking-glasses in which to survey their own."

Among all God's children, there is not one possessed with a dumb devil. Prayerless persons are forsaken of God, blinded by Satan, hardened

in sin, and with every breath they draw, liable
to all temporal, spiritual, and eternal judgments.

There is no such way to attain to greater measures of grace, as for a man to live up to that little grace he has.

Bring your graces to the touchstone, to try
their truth, rather than to the balance to weigh
their measure.

Christ is of all gifts the sweetest gift. As the
tree (Exodus, xv. 25) *sweetened the bitter waters*,
so this gift, the Lord Jesus, of whom that tree
was a type, sweetens all other gifts that are bestowed upon the sons of men. He turns every
bitter into sweet, and makes every sweet more
sweet.

Pride grows with the decrease of other sins,
and thrives by their decay. Satan is subtle; he
will make a man proud of his very graces—he
will make him proud that he is not proud.

There is nothing says one, "that endures so
small a time as the memory of mercies received;

and the more great they are, the more commonly they are recompensed with ingratitude."

It is very observable that the eagle and the lion, those brave creatures, were not offered in sacrifice unto God, but the poor lamb and dove, to denote that God regards not high and lofty spirits; but meek, poor, contemptible spirits God will accept.

"Talk not of a good life," said a heathen, "but let thy life speak." God appointed that the weights and measures of the sanctuary should be twice as large as those of the commonwealth, to show that he expects much more of those that wait upon him in the sanctuary, than he does of others. Christians should be like musk among linen, which casts a fragrant smell; or like that box of spikenard, which being broken open filled the house with its odor.

Impunity oftentimes causes impudency, but forbearance is no acquaintance. The longer the hand is lifted up, the heavier will be the blow at last. Of all metals, lead is the coldest, but being melted, it becomes the hottest. Humble souls know how to apply this, and proud souls shall sooner or later experience this.

It was a sweet saying of one, "O Lord, I have come to thee; but by thee, I will never go from thee, without thee."

Our hearts naturally are like the isle of Patmos, which is so barren of any good, that nothing will grow but in earth that is brought from other places; yet Christ can make them like a watered garden, and like a spring of water whose waters fail not.

The choicest buildings have the lowest foundations; the best balsam sinks to the bottom; those ears of corn and boughs of trees that are most filled and best laden, bow lowest; so do those souls that are most laden with the fruits of paradise.

Souls that are rich in grace, labor after greater measures of grace out of love to grace, and because of an excellency that they see in grace. Grace is a very sparkling jewel, and he who loves it and pursues after it for its own native beauty, has much of it within him.

Mercies make a humble soul glad, but not proud. A humble soul is lowest when his mercies are highest; he is least when he is greatest; he is most poor when he is most rich.

Pride is a sin that will put the soul upon the worst of sins. Pride is a gilded misery, a secret poison, a hidden plague. It is the engineer of deceit, the mother of hypocrisy, the parent of mercy, the moth of holiness, the blinder of hearts, the turner of medicines into maladies, and remedies into diseases.

" *Whereby are given unto us exceeding great and precious promises,*" 2 Peter, i. 4. The promises are a precious book; every leaf drops myrrh and mercy. They are golden vessels, laden with the choicest jewels that heaven can afford, or the soul desire. *There is nothing you can truly call a mercy, but you will find it in the promises.*

Souls that know by experience what the bosom of Christ is what spiritual communion is, and what the glory of heaven is, will not be put off by God or man with things that are mixed, mutable, and momentary. So Luther, a man strong in grace, when he had a gown and money given him by the elector, turned himself about, and said, "I protest, God shall not put me off with these poor low things."

Plutarch reports, that it was wont to be the way of the Molossians, when they would seek the favor of their prince, that they took up the king's son in their arms, and so went and kneeled before the king, and by this means overcame him. So do humble souls make a conquest upon God with Christ in their arms: the Father will not repulse the soul that brings Christ with him.

Katherine Bretterge once after a great conflict with Satan, said, "Reason not with me, I am but a weak woman; if thou hast any thing to say, say it to my Christ, he is my advocate, my strength, and my Redeemer; and he shall plead for me."

Every soul won to Christ is a glorious pearl added to a preacher's crown. They who, by

preaching Christ, win souls to Christ, shall shine
as the stars in the firmament (Daniel, xii. 3).

It is a sad thing when Christians borrow spectacles to behold their weak brethren's weaknesses, and refuse looking glasses wherein they may
see their weak brethren's grace.

Three things are called precious in the Scriptures: "precious faith," (2 Peter, i. 1); "precious promises," (verse 4); "precious blood,"
(1 Peter, i. 19). All our precious mercies twine
to us in precious blood, as may be seen by com-
paring these Scriptures together: Romans, v. 9;
Ephesians, i. 7; Colossians, i. 20; Hebrews, ix.
7, 14; x. 19; 1 John, i. 7; Revelations, i. 5. It
was an excellent saying of Luther, "One little
drop of this blood is more worth than heaven
and earth." Christ's blood is heaven's key.

Well may grace be called *the Divine nature*,
for as God brings light out of darkness, comfort
out of sorrow, riches out of poverty, and glory
out of shame, so does grace bring day out of
night, and sweet out of bitter, and plenty out of
poverty, and glory out of shame. It turns coun-

ters into gold, pebbles into pearls, sickness into health, weakness into strength, and wants into abundance; *having* nothing, and yet possessing all things.

He who is good, is bound to do good; for gifts and graces are given, not only to make us good and keep us good, but also to make us, yea, to provoke us to *do* good. Why has Christ put a box of precious ointment into every Christian's hand, but that it should be opened for the benefit of others?

Pride is Satan's *disease*. It is so base a disease, that God would rather see his dearest children buffeted by Satan, than that in pride they should be like to Satan (2 Corinthians, xii. 7).

He that loveth silver shall not be satisfied with silver; nor he that loveth abundance with increase (Ecclesiastes, v. 10). A man may as soon fill a chest with grace, or a vessel with virtue, as a heart with wealth. If Alexander conquer one world, he will wish for another to conquer.

Sin's murdering morsels will deceive those

who devour them. Many eat *that* on earth, which they digest in hell.

Human doctrines can not cure a wound in the conscience. The remedy is too weak for the disease. Conscience, like the vulture of Prometheus, will still lie gnawing, notwithstanding all that such doctrines can do.

Zeal is like fire: in the chimney it is one of the best servants; but out of the chimney it is one of the worst masters. Zeal, kept by knowledge and wisdom in its proper place, is a choice servant to Christ and the saints; but zeal not bounded by wisdom and knowledge is the highway to undo all, and to make a hell for many at once.

Has God given thee a crown, and wilt thou not trust him for a crumb? Has he given thee a house that *hath foundations, whose builder and maker is God?* Has he given thee a kingdom that shaketh not? And wilt thou not trust him for a cottage, for a little house-room, in this world? Has he given thee himself, his Son, his Spirit, his grace; and wilt thou not trust him to

give thee bread, and friends, and clothes, and
other necessary mercies that he knows thou need-
est? Has he given thee the greater, and will he
stand with thee for the less? Surely not. He
that spared not his own Son, but delivered him
up for us all, how shall he not with him also
freely give us all things? (Romans, viii. 32.)

One asked a philosopher what God was doing;
he answered, that his whole work was to lift up
the humble, and to cast down the proud.

A thankful soul holds consort with the music
of heaven. The little birds do not sip one drop
of water, but they look up as if they meant to
give thanks;—to show us what we should do for
every drop of grace.

The dove made use of her wings to flee to the
ark; so does a humble soul of his duties to flee
to Christ. Though the dove did use her wings,
yet she did not trust in them, but in the ark; so
though a humble soul does use duties, yet he
does not trust in his duties, but in his Jesus.

Dionysius having not very well used Plato at

his court, when he was gone, fearing lest he should write against him, sent after him to bid him not to do so. "Tell Dionysius," says Plato, "that I have not so much leisure as to think of him." So humble, wronged souls are not at leisure to think of the wrongs and injuries that others do them.

The strongest creature, the lion, and the wisest creature, the serpent, if they be dormant, are as easily surprised as the weakest worms. So the strongest and wisest saints, if their graces be asleep, if they be only in the habit and not in the exercise, may be as easily surprised and vanquished as the weakest Christians in all the world: witness David, Solomon, Samson, and Peter. Every enemy insults over him that has lost the use of his weapons.

Grace is a ring of gold, and Christ is the sparkling diamond in that ring.

Weak Christians are very apt to three things —to choose their mercies, to choose their crosses, and to choose their employments.

Oh, how sweet is a harbor after a long storm, and a sunshiny day after a dark and tempestuous night, and a warm spring after a sharp winter! The miseries and difficulties that a man meets with in this world, will exceedingly sweeten the glory of that other world.

"*Add to your faith virtue*," (2 Peter, i. 5). The Greek word that is here rendered, *add*, has a great emphasis in it: it is taken from dancing round. "Link them," says the apostle, "hand in hand." As in dancing, virgins take hand, so we must pin hand to hand in these holy measures and lead up the dance of graces.

Austin says, "If one drop of the joy of the Holy Ghost should fall into hell, it would swallow up all the torments of hell."

"*I know whom I have believed, and am persuaded that he is able to keep that which I have committed unto him against that day*," (2 Timothy, i. 12). The child can not better secure any precious thing it has, than by putting it into the father's hands to keep. Our mercies are always safest and surest when they are out of our hands,

3

and in the hands of God. We trust as we love, and we trust where we love ; where we love much, we trust much ; much trust speaks out much love; if we love Christ much, surely we shall trust him much.

Weak saints are as much united to Christ, as much justified by Christ, as much reconciled by Christ, and as much pardoned by Christ, as the strongest saints. He that looked upon the brazen serpent, though with weak sight, was healed as thoroughly as he that looked upon it with a stronger sight.

If you would have a clear evidence that that little love, that little faith, that little zeal, you have is true, then live up to that love, live up to that faith, live up to that zeal that you have; and this will evidence beyond all contradiction.

Faith has an influence upon all other graces : it is like a silver thread, that runs through a chain of pearls ; it puts strength and vivacity into all other graces.

Gregory calls the Scripture "the heart and

soul of God;" for in the Scriptures, as in a glass, we may see how the heart and soul of God stand towards his poor creatures.

Labor to be rich in grace. A little star yields but a little light, and a little grace will yield but a little comfort; but great measures of grace will yield a man not only a heaven hereafter, but also a heaven of joy here. Divine comfort is a choice flower, a precious jewel, and only to be found in their bosoms who are rich in grace.

Christ dwells in that heart most eminently that hath emptied itself of itself.

" *I will never leave thee nor forsake thee*" (Hebrews, xiii. 5). There are five negatives in the Greek to assure God's people that he will never forsake them. Five times this precious promise is renewed in the Scripture, that we might have the stronger consolation, and that we might press and press it again, till we have gotten all the sweetness out of it.

Augustine said: " Deliver me, O Lord, from that evil man, *myself.*"

Grace is a sweet flower of paradise, a spark of glory.

" He humbled himself." The Sun of Righteousness went ten degrees back in the dial of his Father, that he might come to us with healing under his wings.

" *Woman, thy faith hath made thee whole*" (Luke, viii. 48). Ah! Christians, it is not your trembling, or your falling down, or your sweating in this or that service, that will stop the bloody issue of your sins; but believing in Christ.

All the sighing, mourning, sobbing, and complaining in the world do not so undeniably evidence a man to be humble as his overlooking his own righteousness, and living really and purely upon the righteousness of Christ. This is the greatest demonstration of humility that can be shown by man.

A humble soul is like the violet that by its fragrant smell draws the eye and the heart of others to it.

It was a wise and a Christian speech of Charles the Fifth to the Duke of Venice, who, when he had showed him the glory of his princely palace and earthly paradise, instead of admiring it, or him for it, only returned him this grave and serious memento, "These are the things which make us unwilling to die."

As a humble soul knows that the stars have their situation in heaven, though sometimes he sees them by their reflection in the bottom of a well, or in a ditch; so he knows that godly souls, though never so poor, low, and contemptible, as to the things of this world, are fixed in heaven, in the region above; and therefore their poverty and meanness is no bar to hinder him from learning of them.

Those sins shall never be a Christian's bane that are now his greatest burden. It is not falling into the water, but lying in the water, that drowns. It is not falling into sin, but lying in sin, that destroys the soul. If sin and thy heart are two, Christ and thy heart are one.

Poor men do not live upon themselves, they.

3*

live upon others; they live upon the care of others, the love of others, the provision of others; and thus a humble soul lives upon the care of Christ, the love of Christ, the promise of Christ, the faithfulness of Christ, the discoveries of Christ.

Seneca calls sloth "*the nurse of beggary, the mother of misery.*" And slothful Christians find it so.

The nearer any soul draws to God, the more humble will that soul lie before God. None so near God as the angels, and none so humble before God as the angels.

God scatters giftless gifts, the honors, riches, and favors, of this world, up and down among the worst of men; but as for his gold, his Spirit, his grace, his Son, his favor, these are jewels that he only casts into the bosoms of saints, and that because he dearly loves them.

Much of a Christian's spiritual strength lies in secret prayer, as Samson's did in his hair. Nothing disarms Satan and weakens sin like this.

Secret prayers are the pillars of smoke wherein the soul ascends to God out of the wilderness of this world. Secret prayer is Jacob's ladder, where you have God descending into the soul, and the soul sweetly ascending to God. Secret meals are very fattening, and secret duties are very soul-enriching.

He that drew Alexander whilst he had a scar upon his face, drew him with his finger upon the scar. So when the Lord comes to look upon a poor soul, he lays his finger upon the scar, upon the infirmity, that he may see nothing but grace, which is the beauty and the glory of the soul.

What madness and folly is it, that the favorites of heaven should envy the men of the world, who at best do but feed upon the scraps that come from God's table! Temporals are the bones; spirituals are the marrow. Is it below a man to envy the dogs, because of the bones? And is it not much more below a Christian to envy others for temporals, when himself enjoys spirituals?

The Canaanitish woman, in the 15th of St.

Matthew, sets a high price upon a crumb of
mercy. "Ah! Lord," says the humble soul,
"if I may not have a loaf of mercy, give me a
piece of mercy; if not a piece of mercy, give me
a crumb of mercy. If I may not have sunlight,
let me have moonlight; if not moonlight, let me
have starlight; if not starlight, let me have can-
dle-light; and for that I will bless thee." Faith
will pick an argument out of a repulse, and turn
discouragements into encouragements.

One of the ancients used to say, that humility
is the first, second, and third grace of a Christian.

When you look upon the stream, remember
the fountain; when you look upon the flower,
remember the root; when you look upon the
stars, remember the sun; and when you look
upon your graces, remember the *fountain* of
grace, else Satan will be too hard for you.

All those services are lost, wherein faith has
not a hand. We may write "lost" upon all the
prayers we make, and upon all the sermons we
hear, and upon all the tears we shed, and upon

all the alms we give, if all be not managed by a hand of faith.

"*My sin is ever before me*" (Psalm li. 3). A humble soul sees that he can stay no more from sin, than the heart can from panting, and the pulse from beating. He sees his heart and life to be fuller of sin than the firmament is of stars; and this keeps him low. He sees that sin is so bred in the bone, that till his bones, as Joseph's, be carried out of the Egypt of this world, it will not out. Though sin and grace were never born together, and though they shall not die together, yet while the believer lives, these two must live together; and this keeps him humble.

When Cæsar gave one a great reward, " This," said he, " is too great a gift for me to receive;" but, says Cæsar, " It is not too great a gift for me to give." So, though the least gift that Christ gives, in one sense, is too much for us to receive, yet the greatest gifts are not too great for Christ to give.

"*But go your way, tell his disciples and Peter that he goeth before you into Galilee; there shall ye*

see him, as he said unto you" (Mark, xvi. 7). O
admirable love! O matchless mercy! Where
sin abounds, grace does superabound. This is
the glory of Christ, that he carries it sweetly
towards his people, when they carry themselves
unworthily towards him. Christ looks more
upon Peter's sorrow, than upon his sin; more
upon his tears, than upon his oaths. The Lord
will not cast away weak saints for their great unbelief, because there is a little faith in them. He
will not throw them away for that hypocrisy that
is in them, because of that little sincerity that is
in them. He will not cast away weak saints for
that pride that is in them, because of those rays
of humility that shine in them. He will not despise his people for their passions, because of
those grains of meekness that are in them. A
wise man will not throw away a little gold, because of a great deal of dross that cleaves to it;
nor a little wheat, because mixed with much
chaff; and will God? will God?

Grace is a ring of gold, and Christ is the pearl
in that ring; and he that looks more upon the
ring than the pearl that is in it, in the hour of
temptation will certainly fall. When the wife's

eye is upon her rings or jewels, then her heart
must be set upon her husband. When grace is
in the eye, Christ must at that time be in the
arms. *Christ*, and not grace, must lie nearest to
a Christian's heart.

Here God gives his people some taste, that they
may not faint; and he gives them but a taste,
that they may long to be at home, that they may
keep humble, that they may sit loose from things
below, that they may not break and despise
bruised reeds, and that heaven may be more
sweet to them at last.

Grace grows by exercise, and decays by dis-
use. Though both arms grow, yet that which a
man most uses is the stronger; so it is both in
gifts and graces. In birds, the wings which have
been used most, are sweetest: the application is
easy.

Christ is a most precious commodity, he is better than rubies or the most costly pearls; and
we must part with our old gold, with our shining
gold, our old sins, our most shining sins, or we
must perish for ever. Christ is to be sought and

bought with any pains, at any price; we can not buy this gold too dear. He is a jewel more worth than a thousand worlds, as all know who have him. Get him, and get all; miss him and miss all.

" *The light and glory of humble Christians rises by degrees*" (Canticles, vi. 10). *Looking forth as the morning*, with a little light; *fair as the moon*, more light; *clear as the sun*, coming up to a still higher degree of spiritual light, life, and glory.

All the arrows that are shot at a Christian, stick in his buckler; they never reach his conscience, his soul. The raging waves beat sorely against Noah's ark, but they touched not him.

Faith is the champion of grace, and love the nurse; but humility is the beauty of grace. *Be clothed with humility.* The Greek word imports that humility is the ribbon or string that ties together all those precious pearls, the rest of the graces. If this string break, they are all scattered.

The Lord Jesus shares with saints in their afflictions. " *In all their afflictions he was afflicted, and the angel of his presence saved them*" (Isaiah, lxiii. 9). It is between Christ and his Church, as between two lute-strings—no sooner one is struck, but the other trembles.

It was a sweet observation of Luther, " That for the most part when God set him upon any special service for the good of the Church, he was brought low by some fit of sickness or other." Surely, as the lower the ebb, the higher the tide; so the lower any descend in humility, the higher they shall ascend in honor and glory. The lower this foundation of humility is laid, the higher shall the roof of honor be overlaid.

Great measures of grace carry with them the greatest evidence of a man's union and communion with God; and the more a man's union and communion with God are evidenced, the more will the soul be filled with that joy which is unspeakable and full of glory, and with that comfort and peace which pass understanding. In great measures of grace, as in a crystal glass, the soul sees the glorious face of God shining and sparkling, and this fills the soul with joy.

4

" *Who maketh thee to differ from another?   And what hast thou that thou hast not received?*" (1 Corinthians, iv. 7.)   Thou talkest of light, of love, of fear, of faith : but what are all these but pearls of glory, that are freely given thee by the hand of grace?

Every good and every perfect gift cometh down from above.   The greatest excellencies in us do as much depend on God, as the light does upon the sun.   When thou lookest upon thy wisdom thou must say, " Here is wisdom, but it is *from above.*   Here is some weak love working towards Christ, but it is *from above.*   Here is joy, and comfort, and peace, but these are all the flowers of paradise; they never grow in nature's garden."   When a soul looks thus upon all those costly diamonds with which his heart is decked, he keeps low, though his graces are high.

A humble soul can not, a humble soul dares not, call any thing little that has Christ in it; neither can a humble soul call or count any thing great wherein he sees not Chr'st, wherein he enjoys not Christ.

God looks more upon the bright side of the cloud than the dark. "*Remember the patience of Job*" (James, v. 11). It is not "Remember the murmuring of Job, the cursing of Job, the complainings of Job, the impatience of Job," but "*Remember the patience of Job.*" God looks upon the pearl and not upon the spot that is in it. So in Hebrews, xi. 30, 31, there is mention made of Rahab's faith, love, and peaceable behavior towards the spies; but no mention made of her lie. The Lord overlooks her weakness, and keeps his eye upon her virtues. Where God sees but a little grace, he does, as it were, hide his eyes from those circumstances that might seem to deface the glory of it.

The picture of a dear friend is not to be thrust into a corner, but placed in some conspicuous part in the house: so our graces are the very image of Christ; they are his picture, and therefore to be held forth to open view.

As there are no mercies equal to spiritual mercies, so there are no judgments equal to spiritual judgments. Oh! the slightness, the coldness, the deadness, the barrenness, that are abroad in the world! God suits his judgments to men's sins; the greatest sins are always attended with the greatest judgments. In *these days* men sin against more glorious means, more great love, more clear light, more tender bowels of mercy, than formerly; and therefore God gives men up to more sad and dreadful spiritual judgments than formerly.

Little sins (suppose them so) are very dangerous. A little leaven leaveneth the whole lump; a little staff may kill one; a little leak in a ship sinks it; a little flaw in a good cause mars it; so a little sin may at once bar the door of heaven, and open the gates of hell; though the scorpion be little, yet will it sting a lion to death; and so will the least sin, if not pardoned by the death of Christ.

Earthly riches are called thorns, and well they may be; for, as thorns, they pierce both head and heart; the head with cares in getting them, and the heart with grief in parting with them.

Things satisfy as they suit. There is a good, and there is a suitable good; now it is only the suitable good that satisfies the soul of a man. A pardon is most suitable to a condemned man, and therefore it best satisfies him. Health is most suitable to the sick, and therefore it satisfies when it is attained. As bread satisfies the hungry soul, and drink the thirsty soul, and clothing the naked soul, so do the precious gifts that Christ bestows upon the soul satisfy the soul.

There was a holy man that rarely heard of other men's crimson sins, but he usually bedewed the place with his tears, considering that the seeds of those very sins were in his own nature. In thy nature thou hast that which would lead thee, with the Pharisees, to oppose Christ, and, with Judas, to betray Christ; and, with Pilate, to condemn Christ; and, with the soldiers, to crucify Christ. Oh! what a monster wouldst thou prove, should God but leave thee to act suitably to that sinful and woful nature of thine.

"*We walk by faith and not by sight*" (2 Corinthians, v. 7). Christians, you must remember that it is one thing for God to love you, and another thing for God to tell you that he loves you. Your *happiness* lies in the first, your *com-*

fort in the second. God has stopped his ears against the prayers of many a precious soul whom he has dearly loved. And, verily, he who makes sense and carnal reason a judge of his condition, will be happy and miserable, blessed and cursed, saved and lost, many times in a day, yea, in an hour.

Luther says, " When my heart is coldest and highest, I present God to my soul under the notions of his greatness; but when my heart is loose and fearing, then I present God to my soul under the notion of his goodness.

Jesus Christ has the greatest worth and wealth in him. As the worth and value of many pieces of silver is in one piece of gold, so all the heavenly excellencies that are scattered abroad in angels and men are united in Christ; yea, all the whole volume of perfection, which is spread through heaven and earth, is epitomised in Christ.

The altar under the law was hollow, to receive the fire, the wood, and the sacrifice; so the hearts of men under the Gospel must be humble, empty of all spiritual pride and self-conceitedness, that so they may receive the fire of the Spirit, and Jesus Christ, who offered himself a sacrifice for our sins.

There is no way to avoid perishing by Christ's iron rod, but by kissing his golden scepter.

Christ did not die all at once upon the cross, but by little and little: to show us that his death should extend to the slaying of sin gradually in the souls of the saints.

Satan is so artificial, so subtle and critical, that he can make our very graces to serve him against our graces; conquering joy by joy, sorrow by sorrow, humility by humility, fear by fear, love by love, if we do not look upon all our graces as streams flowing from the fountain above, and as fruits growing upon the tree of life that is in the midst of the Paradise of God. Therefore when one eye is fixed upon our graces, let the other be always fixed upon the God of grace.

A humble heart is an aspiring heart. It can not be contented to get up some rounds in Jacob's ladder, but it must get to the very top of the ladder, to the very top of holiness. Verily, heaven is for that man, and that man is for heaven, who sets up for his mark the perfection of holiness.

Some say that roses grow the sweeter when they are planted by garlic. Verily, Christians who have gloriously improved their graces, are like those roses; they grow sweeter and sweeter, holier and holier, by wicked men. The best diamonds shine most in the dark, and so do the best Christians shine most in the worst times.

No knowledge humbles and abases like that which is inward and experimental. It is a sad thing to be often eating of the tree of knowledge, but never to taste of the tree of life. As the sun is necessary to the world, the eye to the body, the pilot to the ship, the general to the army; so is experimental knowledge to the humbling of a soul.

In heaven there are no prayers, but all praises. I am apt to think that there can not be a clearer nor a greater argument of a man's right to heaven and ripeness for heaven, than this—being much in the work of heaven here on earth. There is no grace but love, and no duty but thankfulness, that goes with us to heaven.

Many saints have had their hearts warmed and heated by sttting near other saints' fires, by eyeing and dwelling upon other saints' graces. When men's graces shine as Moses' face did— when their lives, as one speaks of Joseph's life, is a very heaven, sparkling with variety of virtues as with so many bright stars—ah! how are others stirred up to glorify God, and to cry out, "These are Christians indeed ; these are an honor to their God, a crown to their Christ, and a credit to their gospel."

Sin and grace are like two buckets at a well— when one is up, the other is down ; they are like the two laurels at Rome—when one flourishes, the other withers. Certainly, the readiest and the surest way to bring under the power of sin, is to be much in the exercise of grace.

Of all the graces that be in the soul of man, faith is the most useful grace; and therefore above all, labor to be rich in faith. It is a Christian's right eye, without which he can not *look* for Christ; it is his right hand, without which he can not *do* for Christ; it is his tongue, without which he can not *speak* for Christ; it is his vital spirits, without which he can not act for Christ.

Count Anhalt, that princely preacher, was wont to say, "that the whole Scriptures were the swaddling bands of the child Jesus, he being to be found almost in every page, in every verse, in every line."

The only way to avoid cannon-shot is to fall down. No such way to be freed from temptations as to keep low.

He that escapes reprehension, may suspect his adoption. God had one Son without corruption, but no son without correction.

There is no such way to get much grace, as to be thankful for a little grace. He who opens his mouth wide in praises, shall have his heart filled with graces. Ingratitude stops the ear of God, and shuts the hand of God, and turns away the heart of the God of grace; and therefore we had need to be thankful for a little grace.

Satan's greatest plot is to weaken the faith of Christians. "*And the Lord said, Simon, Simon, behold, Satan hath desired to have you, that he may sift you as wheat ; but I have prayed for thee, that thy faith fail not*" (Luke, xxii. 31, 32). Satan has an aching tooth at thy faith; his design is upon that; he will labor might and main to weaken that, to frustrate that; and therefore I have prayed that thy faith fail not.

As a poor man lives and deals upon the credits of others, so does a humble soul live and deal with God, for the strengthening of every grace, and for the supply of every mercy upon the credit of the Lord Jesus. He knows that since he broke with God in innocency, God will trust him no more, he will take his word no more; and therefore when he goes to God for mercy, he brings his Benjamin, his Jesus, in his arms, and pleads for mercy upon the account of Jesus.

Some Christians as are like to Pharaoh's lean kine, reproach three at once—God, the Gospel, and their teachers; and this age is full of such Christians.

Pride sets a man in opposition against God. Other sins are aversions from God, but this sin is a coming against God. In other sins a man flies *from* God, but in this sin a man flies *upon* God. " *God resisteth the proud*" (James, iv. 6).

No saint so like a sinner, as a weak saint.

None are such objects of scorn and envy, as those who have most of Christ within. Envy does ever ascend: it never descends.

None so much in the school of temptation as those who are most rich in grace. There are none who are such blocks, such mountains in Satan's way, as these; none do him that mischief as these; none are so active and so resolute in their oppositions against him, as these; and therefore none so assaulted and tempted as these.

Whatever gift of God in man brings him within the compass of God's promise of eternal mercy, that gift must be an infallible evidence of salvation and happiness.

A real sense of our own unworthiness renders

us most fit for divine mercy. This objection, "I am unworthy," is an unworthy objection, and speaks out much pride and ignorance of the Gospel, and of the freeness and riches of God's grace.

Carnal reason is an enemy to faith : it is ever crossing and contradicting it. It will never be well with thee, Christian, so long as thou art swayed by carnal reason, and reliest more upon thy five senses, than upon the four Evangelists. As the body lives by breathing, so the soul lives by believing.

Though grace is a glorious creature, it is but a creature, and therefore must be upheld by its Creator. Though grace be a beautiful child, yet it is but a child, that must be upheld by the father's arms. This, Christians, you must remember, and give glory to God.

Luther confesses that, before his conversion, he met not with a more displeasing word, in all the study of divinity, than the word *repent*, but after the Lord had converted him, and manifested himself to him, he delighted in this word;

5

then he could sorrow for his sins, and rejoice in his sorrow.

The number of difficulties makes the Christian's conquest the more illustrious. A gracious man should be made up all of fire, overcoming and consuming all opposition, as fire does the stubble. All difficulties should be but whetstones to his fortitude.

A humble soul is quick-sighted: he sees the rod in a father's hand; he sees honey upon the top of every twig; and so can bless God; he sees sugar at the bottom of the bitterest cup that God doth put into his hands; he knows that God's house of correction is a school of instruction; and so he can sit down and bless when the rod is upon his back.

Such as have made a considerable improvement of their gifts and graces, have hearts as large as their heads; whereas most men's heads have outgrown their hearts.

A Christian should be like the lamp in the story, that never went out. Were it not for the sun, it would be perpetual night in the world, notwithstanding all starlight, and torchlight, and moonlight. It is not the torchlight of natural parts and creature comforts, nor the starlight of civil honesty and common gifts, nor yet the moonlight of temporary faith and formal profession, that can make day in the soul, till the Sun of Righteousness arise and shine upon it.

"What a shame is it," says Hierome, "that faith should not be able to do that which infidelity has done!" What, not better fruit in the vineyard, in the garden of God, than in the wilderness? What, not better fruit grow upon the tree of life, than upon the root of nature?

Every thing that a man leans upon but God, will be a dart that will certainly pierce his heart through and through. He who leans only upon Christ, lives the highest, choicest, safest, and sweetest life.

Luther would often say he had rather that all his books should be burnt, than that they should be a means to hinder persons from studying the Scripture.

Every one should strive to be like to them in grace whom they desire to be equal with in glory. He that shoots at the sun, though he be far short, will shoot higher than he who aims at a shrub. It is best, and it speaks out much of Christ within, to eye the highest and the worthiest examples.

It is a proof that a man is grown higher when he can reach higher than he could before; so it is an argument that a soul is grown rich in grace when it can reach beyond what formerly it could reach unto; when in duty, it can reach above duty; when in an ordinance, it can reach to Christ above the ordinance; when under enlargements, it can reach above enlargements to Jesus Christ.

Anselm used to say that if he should see the shame of sin on the one hand and the pains of hell on the other, and must of necessity choose one, he would rather be thrust into hell without sin than go into heaven with sin; so great was his hatred and detestation of sin.

" *They shall look upon me whom they have*

pierced, and they shall mourn for him" (Zechariah, xii. 10). All Gospel mourning flows from believing; they shall first look, and then mourn. All who know any thing, know this, that "*Whatever is not of faith, is sin.*" Till men have faith in Christ, their best services are but glorious sins.

Corruption in the heart, when it breaks forth, is like a breach in the sea, which begins in a narrow passage, till it eats through and casts down all before it. The debates of the soul are quick and soon ended, and that may be done in a moment which may undo a man for ever.

"*In every thing give thanks*" (1 Thessalonians, v. 18). The language of a humble soul is, If it be thy will that I should be in darkness, I will bless thee; and if it be thy will that I should be again in light, I will bless thee; if thou wilt comfort me, I will bless thee, and if thou wilt afflict me, I will bless thee; if thou wilt make me poor, I will bless thee; if thou wilt make me rich, I will bless thee; if thou wilt give me the least mercy, I will bless thee; if thou wilt give me no mercy, I will bless thee.

God is most angry when he shows no anger. God keep us from this mercy. This kind of mercy is worse than all other kind of misery.

Thoughts are the first-born, the blossoms of the soul, the beginning of our strength, whether for good or evil, and they are the greatest evidences for or against a man that can be.

The senate of Rome accounted it a diminution of Augustus Cæsar's dignity to join any consuls with him for the better carrying on of the affairs of the state. Oh! but our God does not think it a diminution of his dignity that even his poor despised servants should be fellow-laborers and co-workers with him in the salvation of souls.

Humility can not find three things on this side heaven : it can not find fullness in the creature, or sweetness in sin, or life in an ordinance without Christ; but it always finds these three things on this side heaven: the soul to be empty, Christ to be full, and every mercy and duty to be sweet wherein Christ is enjoyed.

Afflictions are called by some "the mother

of virtue." Manasseh's chain was more profitable to him than his crown. Luther could not understand some Scriptures till he was in affliction.

No vessels that God delights so much to fill as broken vessels, contrite spirits. *"He resisteth the proud and giveth grace to the humble"* (James, iv. 6). The silver dews flow down from the mountains to the lowest valleys. A humble soul that lies low, oh, what sights of God has he! what glory does he behold, when the proud soul sees nothing! He that is in the low pits and caves of the earth sees the stars in the firmament, when they who are upon the tops of the mountains discern them not.

A Christian's graces are but Christ's picture, Christ's image, and, therefore, do not you worship his image, and, in the meanwhile, neglect his person. Make much of his picture, but make more of himself; let his picture have your eye, but let himself have your heart.

" I know not," says one, " whether the maintenance of the least sin be not worse than the commission of the greatest; for this may be of frailty, that argues obstinacy. One little miscarriage in the eyes of the world overshadows all a Christian's graces, as one cloud sometimes overshadows the whole body of the sun.

Our hearts carry the greatest stroke in every sin. Satan can never undo a man without himself; but a man may easily undo himself without Satan.

The most holy men are always the most humble men; none so humble on earth as those that live highest in heaven.

Mr. Fox used to say that, as he got much good by his sins, so he got much hurt by his graces.

Christians, remember this, that your strength to stand and overcome must not be expected from graces received, but from the fresh and renewed influences of heaven. You must lean more upon Christ than upon your duties; you must lean more upon Christ than upon spiritual tastes and discoveries; you must lean more upon

Christ than upon your graces; or else Satan will lead you into captivity.

"*Nor quench the smoking flax*" (Matthew, xii. 20). The wick of a candle is little worth, and yet less when it smokes, yielding neither light nor heat, but rather offends with an ill smell, which men can not bear, but will tread it out. But the Lord Jesus Christ will not do so. Souls whose knowledge, love, faith, and zeal, do but smoke out, the Lord Jesus will not trample under foot; nay, he will cherish, nourish, and strengthen such to life eternal.

If all Christians should be rich in all graces, what difference would there be between heaven and earth? what need would there be of ordinances? and when would Christians long to be dissolved, and to be with Christ?

"*Now I know in part, but then shall I know even as I also am known*" (1 Corinthians, xiii. 12), Christians know but little of what they should know; they know but little of what they might know; they know but little of what others know; they know but little of what they desire to know;

they know but little of what they shall know, when they shall come to know even as they are known; and these weak and imperfect glimpses that they have of God and heaven here, are infallible pledges of that perfect knowledge and full prospect which they shall have of God and heaven hereafter. That little spark of joy is an earnest of those everlasting delights which shall be theirs when all sorrow and mourning shall flee away; and those sips of comfort are but foretastes of that river of everlasting pleasures which is at God's right hand.

Some degree of comfort follows every good action; as heat accompanies fire; as beams and influences issue from the sun.

Guilt or grief is all that gracious souls get by communion with vain souls.

"It is with truth," said Melancthon, "as it is with holy water, every one praises it, and thinks it has some rare virtue in it; but offer to sprinkle them with it, and they will shut their eyes, and turn away their faces from it."

Sometimes grace in a rugged, unhewn nature is like a gold ring on a leprous hand, or a diamond set in iron, or a jewel in a swine's snout.

The stars which have least circuit are nearest the pole; and men who are least perplexed with business, are commonly nearest to God.

Christ was born in an inn, to show that he receives all comers; his garments were divided into four parts, to show that out of what parts of the world soever we come, we shall be received.

He that fights against Satan, in the strength of his own resolutions, constitution, or education, will certainly fly and fall before him: Satan will be too hard for such a soul, and lead him captive at his pleasure. The only way to stand, conquer, and triumph, is still to plead, "*It is written*," as Christ did. There is no sword, but the two-edged sword of the Spirit, that will be found to be mettle of proof, when a soul comes to engage against Satan.

Hard weather tries what health we have;

afflictions try what sap we have, what grace we
have. Withered leaves soon fall off in windy
weather; rotten boughs quickly break with heavy
weights.

It is said of Cæsar, that he had greater care of
his books than of his royal robes: for swimming
through the water to escape his enemies, he carried his books in his hand above the water, but
lost his robes. What are Cæsar's books to God's
book?

Faith can not be lost, but assurance may;
therefore assurance is not faith. Though assurance is a precious flower in the garden of a saint,
and is more infinitely sweet and delightful to the
soul than all outward comforts and contents, yet
it is but a flower that is subject to fade, and to
lose its freshness and beauty, as saints by sad experience find.

Let your souls dwell upon the vanity of all
things here below, till your hearts are so thoroughly convinced and persuaded of their vanity
of them, as to trample upon them. and make

them a footstool for Christ to get up and ride in a holy triumph in your hearts.

When men have poor, low, light, slight, thoughts of God in their drawing near to God, they tempt the devil to bestir himself, and to cast in a multitude of vain thoughts to disturb and distract the soul in its waiting on God.

It was a saying of Austin, "He that willingly takes from my good name, unwillingly adds to my reward."

The less the temptation is to sin, the greater is that sin. Little sins carry with them but little temptation to sin, and then a man shows most viciousness and unkindness when he sins on a little temptation.

The best men's souls in this life hang between the flesh and the spirit, as it were, like Mohammed's tomb at Mecca, between two lode stones; like Erasmus, as the papists paint him, between heaven and hell; like the tribe of Manasseh, half on this side Jordan, in the land of the Amorites, and half on that side in the holy land;

yet in the issue they shall overcome the flesh, and trample upon the necks of their spiritual enemies.

He that turns not from every sin, turns not aright from any one sin.

The flowers smell sweetest after a shower; vines bear the better for bleeding; the walnut tree is most fruitful when most beaten; so saints spring and thrive most internally when they are most externally afflicted.

Bodia had a story concerning a great rebel who had made a strong party againt a Roman emperor. The emperor makes proclamation that whoever could bring the rebel, dead or alive, he should have a great sum of money. The rebel hearing of this, comes and presents himself before the emperor, and demands the sum of money. "Now," says the emperor, "if I should put him to death, the world would say I did it to save my money." Ah, sinners, shall a heathen do this who had but a drop of mercy and compassion in him; and will not Christ do much more, who has all fullness of grace, mercy and glory in himself? Surely his bowels do yearn toward the worst of rebels.

When Demosthenes was asked what was the first part of an orator, what the second, and what the third, he answered, "Action." The same may I say if any should ask me what is the first, the second, the third part of a Christian, I must answer, "Action." Luther says that "he had rather obey than work miracles." Obedience is better than sacrifice.

He that, to avoid a greater sin, will yield to a lesser, ten thousand to one but God, in justice, will leave that soul to fall into a greater. If we commit one sin to avoid another, it is just we should avoid neither, we having not law nor power in our own hands to keep off sin as we please ; and we, by yielding to the less, do tempt the tempter to tempt us to the great.

As the water lifted up Noah's ark nearer heaven, and as all the stones that were about Stephen's ears did but knock him the closer to Christ, the corner stone, so all the strange, rugged providences that we meet with shall raise us nearer heaven and knock us nearer to Christ, that precious corner stone.

Luther reports of Staupicius, a German minister, that he acknowledged himself that before he came to understand aright the free and powerful grace of God that he vowed and resolved a hundred times against some particular sin, and never could get power over it; at last he saw the reason to be his trusting to his own resolutions; therefore be skillful in the word of righteousness, and in the actings of faith upon Christ and his victory, and that crown of glory that is set before you, and Satan will certainly fly from you.

Satan works most strongly on the fancy when the soul is drowsy. The soul's security is Satan's opportunity to fall upon the soul and to spoil the soul, as Joshua did the men of Ai.

You may as soon fill a bag with wisdom, a chest with virtue, or a circle with a triangle, as the heart of man with any thing here below. A man may have enough of the world to sink him, but he can never have enough to satisfy him.

Socrates said of his enemies, " They may kill me, but they can not hurt me." So afflictions may kill us, but they can not hurt us; they may take away my life, but they can not take away my God, my Christ, my crown.

What is the reason that the angels in heaven have not so much as an idle thought? It is because they are filled with the fullness of God. Take it for an experienced truth, the more the soul is filled with the fullness of God, and enriched with spiritual and heavenly things, the less room there is in that soul for vain thoughts. The fuller the vessel is of wine, the less room there is for water.

God is like a prince that sends not his army against rebels before he has sent his pardon, and proclaimed it by a herald of arms. He first hangs out the white flag of mercy; if this wins men in, they are happy for ever; but if they stand out, then God will put forth his red flag of justice and judgment. If the one is despised, the other shall be felt with a witness.

"Now when Jesus was risen early the first day

6*

*of the week, he appeared first to Mary Magdalene,
out of whom he had cast seven devils*" (Mark xvi.
9). Jansenius says, " It is very observable that
our Saviour, after the resurrection, first appeared
to Mary Magdalene and Peter, who •had been
grievous sinners, in order that even the worst
of sinners may be comforted and encouraged to
come to Christ, to believe in Christ, to rest and
stay their souls upon Christ, for mercy here and
glory hereafter.

Sorrow attends worldly joy, danger attends
worldly safety, loss attends worldly labors, tears
attend worldly purposes. As to these things,
men's hopes are vain, their sorrow certain, and
their joy feigned. The apostle calls this world *a
sea of glass*—a sea for the trouble of it, and glass
for the brittleness and bitterness of it.

Usually, the worst of men have most of all outward things, and the best of men have least of
earth, though most of heaven.

I have read of a fountain that at noonday is
cold, and at midnight it grows warm; so many
a precious soul is cold Godward, and heaven-

ward, and holinessward, in the day of prosperity, that grow warm Godward, and heavenward, and holinessward in the midnight of
adversity

Riches, though well got, are yet but like to
manna : those that gathered less had no want,
and those that gathered more found it but a
trouble and annoyance to them.

Erasmus tells of one who collected all the
lame and defective verses in Flower's works,
but passed over all that were excellent. Oh!
that this were not the practice of many who will
at last meet in heaven—that they were not careful and skillful to collect all the weaknesses of
others, and to pass over all those things that
are excellent in them !

A saint's conflict is against sin universally,
the least as well as the greatest. He looks upon
one sin, and sees that that threw down Noah,
the most righteous man in the world ; and he
looks upon another sin, and sees that that cast
down Abraham, the greatest believer in the
world ; and he looks upon another sin, and sees

that that threw down David, the best king in the world; and he looks upon another sin, and sees that that cast down Paul, the greatest apostle in the world: he sees that one sin threw down Samson, the strongest man in the world; another cast down Solomon, the wisest man in the world; and another Moses, the meekest man in the world; and another sin cast down Job, the most patient man in the world; and this raiseth a holy indignation against all, so that nothing can satisfy and content him but a destruction of all those lusts and vices that vex and rack his righteous soul.

There are some diseases that are called the reproaches of physicians: and there are some people that may be truly called the reproaches of ministers; and these are they who are great hearers, and talkers, and admirers of ministers, but never obey the doctrines delivered by them.

Sinner, remember this: there is no way on earth effectually to be rid of the guilt, filth and power of sin but by believing in a Saviour. It is not resolving, it is not complaining, it is not mourning, but believing, that will make thee divinely victorious over that body of sin that to this day is too strong for thee, and that will certainly be thy ruin if it be not ruined by a hand of faith.

As men take no hold on the arm of flesh till they let go the arm of God, so men take no hold on error till they have let go their hold of truth ; therefore, hold fast the truth.

"Repentance," says a holy man, "strips us naked of all the garments of the old Adam, and leaves not so much as a rag behind;" in this rotten building it leaves not a stone upon a stone. As the flood drowned Noah's own friends and servants, so must the flood of repenting tears drown our sweetest and most profitable sins.

True grace will enable a man to step over the world's crown to take up Christ's cross ; to prefer the cross of Christ above the glory of this world. Godfrey, first king of Jerusalem, refused to be crowned with a crown of gold, saying that it became not a Christian there to wear a crown of gold where Christ had worn a crown of thorns.

Those who through curious wiseness disdain the stately plainness of the Scripture, would do well to remember that God the Father, the great Master of Speech, when he spake from heaven, made use of three several texts of Scripture in one breath: *"This is my beloved Son, in whom I am well pleased, hear ye him"* (Matt. xvii. 5). They are to be found in Psalm ii. 7, Isaiah, xvlii. 1, and Deut. xviii. 15.

No souls fall so low into hell, if they fall, as those souls that, by a hand of mercy, are lifted up nearest to heaven.

Comfort is not of the *being*, but of the *well-being* of a Christian. The best men's joys are as glass, bright and brittle, and evermore in danger of breaking. Spiritual joy is a sun that is often clouded.

Mercy is " Alpha," justice is " Omega."

A Jewish rabbi pressing the practice of re-

pentance upon his disciples, exhorted them to be
sure to repent the day before they died.   One
of them replied that the day of any man's death
was very uncertain.   "Repent, therefore, every
day," said the rabbi, "and then you will be sure
to repent the day before you die."   You who
are wise will know how to apply this to your
own advantage.

Unity is the best bond of safety in every
church and commonwealth.   We shall be invincible, if we be inseparable.   And this did the
Scythian king in Plutarch represent livelily to
his eighty sons.   He, being ready to die, commanded a bundle of arrows fast bound together
to be given to his sons to break ; they all tried
to break them, but being bound fast together,
they could not ; then he caused the band to be
cut, and then they broke them with ease.   He
applied it thus : "My sons, so long as you keep
together, you will be invincible ; but if the band ·
of union be broken betwixt you, you will easily
be broken in pieces."

Christians, bear your faithful ministers upon
your hearts when you are wrestling with God.

*They can tell when they want your prayers, and
when they enjoy your prayers.* Did you pray
more for them, they might do more for your internal and eternal good than now they do.

The three tongues that were written upon the
cross—Greek, Latin and Hebrew—to witness
Christ to be the king of the Jews, do each of
them, in their several idioms, avouch this singular axiom, that Christ is an all-sufficient Saviour; and a threefold cord is not easily broken.

Some are brought to Christ by fire, storms
and tempests; others by more easy and gentle
gales of the Spirit. The Spirit is free in the
work of conversion, and as the wind, it blows
when, where and how it pleases. Thrice happy
are those souls that are brought to Christ,
whether it be in a winter's night, or on a summer's day.

Little sins multiplied, become great. There
is nothing less than a grain of sand—there is
nothing heavier than the sand of the sea when
multiplied.

Love is a golden key to let in Christ, and a strong lock to keep out others; though many may knock at love's door, yet love will open to none but Christ.

It is an honor to be good betimes. A young saint is like the morning star: he is like a pearl in a gold ring. Among all the disciples, John was the youngest, and the most and best beloved.

Severinus, the Indian saint, under the power of assurance, was heard to say, "O my God! do not for pity so overjoy me. If I must still live, and have such consolations, take me to heaven."

After the Roman generals had gotten the victory over their enemies, the senate used not *one* way, but *many* ways, to express their love to them: so after our faith has gotten the victory over Satan, God usually takes the soul in his arms, and courts it, and shows much kindness to it.

A good conscience will look through the blackest clouds, and see a smiling God. Look, as an evil conscience is attended with the greatest fears and doubts, so a good conscience is attended with the greatest clearness and sweetness.

A murmurer is an hieroglyphic of folly; he is a comprehensive vanity; he is a man, and no man; he is sottish and senseless; he neither understands God nor himself, nor any thing as he should (Isaiah, iii. 8).

The Bible is a Christian's magna charta, his chief evidence for heaven. Men highly prize and carefully keep their charters, privileges, conveyances, and assurances of their lands: and shall not the saints much more highly prize, and carefully keep in the closet of their hearts, the precious word of God, which is to them instead of all assurances for their maintainance, deliverance, protection, confirmation, consolation, and eternal salvation?

Where God refuses to correct, there God resolves to destroy. There is no man so near the edge, so near the flames, so near hell, as he whom God will not so much as spend a rod upon. Jerome, writing to a sick friend, has this expression: "I account it a part of unhappiness not to know adversity. I judge you to be miserable, because you have not been miserable." "Nothing," says another, "seems more unhappy to me, than he to whom no adversity has happened."

The soul is the breath of God, the beauty of man, the wonder of angels, and the envy of devils. The soul is a greater miracle in a man, than all the miracles wrought among men. It is not in the power of any outward troubles and afflictions that a Christian meets with, to reach his soul; and therefore he may well sit mute under the smarting rod.

The best and sweetest flowers of Paradise God gives to his people when they are upon their knees. Prayer is the gate of heaven, a key to let us in to Paradise.

Assurance is a mercy too good for most men's hearts; it is a crown too weighty for most men's heads. Assurance is the best and greatest mercy, and therefore God will give it to his best and dearest friends only.

He that lives without assurance, lives upon

some creature enjoyment more than upon God, and so gratifies Satan.

Prayer crowns God with the honor and glory that are due to his name, and God crowns prayer with assurance and comfort. Usually the most praying souls are the most assured souls.

The ball in the emblem says, "The harder you beat me down, the higher I shall bound towards heaven;" so afflictions do but elevate and raise a saint's affections to heaven and heavenly things.

Many men's love to Christ is like the morning dew; it is like Jonah's gourd, that came up in a night, and perished in a night; but that love which accompanies salvation is like Ruth's love, a lasting and an abiding love.

It is sad to see a man fight against his friends; it is sadder to see him fight against his relations; it is saddest of all to see him fight against his prayers. And yet this every Christian does, who murmurs and mutters when the rod of God is upon him.

As our greatest good comes through the sufferings of Christ, so God's greatest glory that he hath from his saints comes through their sufferings.

Weak souls, remember this—as Joseph sent chariots to bring his father and his brethren to him, so God would have your weak graces to be as chariots to bring you to himself, who is the strengthener, cherisher, and increaser of grace.

Backsliding is a wounding sin. We read of no arms for the back, though we do for the breast. He that is but seemingly good, will prove at last exceedingly bad, *will wax worse and worse* (2 Timothy, iii. 13).

Christian, though the cup is bitter, yet it is put into your hand by your Father; though the cross is heavy, yet he that has laid it on your shoulders will bear the heaviest end of it himself; and why then should you murmur?

As every precious stone has virtue in it, so has every promise; and upon these precious promises, precious faith looks and lives; from these it draws comfort and sweetness.

Waiting times are times wherein God is pleased to give his people some sweet tastes of his love, and to lift up the light of his countenance upon them.

Hope takes fast hold of heaven itself. A Christian's hope is not like that of Pandora, which may fly out of the box, and bid the soul farewell, as the hope of the hypocrite does; no, it is like the morning light, the least beam of it shall go on into a complete sunshine; it shall shine forth brighter and brighter till the perfect day.

Every murmurer is his own martyr; he is a murderer: he kills many at once, his joy, his comfort, his peace, his rest, his soul.

The *being* of grace makes our estates safe and sure; the *seeing* of grace makes our lives sweet and comfortable.

The naturalists observe that the pearl, by the

frequent beating of the sun's beams upon it, becomes radiant; so the often beating and shining of the Sun of Righteousness, with his divine beams, upon the saints, causes them to glitter and shine in holiness, righteousness, heavenly mindedness, and humbleness.

Were riches ever true to them that trusted them? As the bird hops from twig to twig, so do riches hop from man to man.

As there is no blood that saves souls like the blood of Christ, so there is no blood that sinks souls like the blood of Christ. A drop of this blood upon a man's *head* at last will make him miserable for ever; but a drop of it upon a man's heart at last will make him happy for ever.

David's heart was more often out of tune than his harp. He begins many of his psalms sighing, and ends them singing; and others he begins in joy and ends in sorrow. "So that one would think," says Peter Moulin, "that those psalms had been composed by two men of a contrary humor."

A man may be truly holy, and yet not have assurance that he shall be eternally happy. His estate may be good, and yet he not see it; he may be in a *safe* condition when he is not in a comfortable condition. All may be well with him in a court of glory, when he would give a thousand worlds that all were but well in the court of conscience.

Luther prized the Word at such a high rate that he said, "he would not live in Paradise, if he might, without the Word; but with the Word he could live in hell itself."

Where the disease is strong, the physic must be strong, or else the cure will never be wrought. God is a wise physician, and he would never give strong medicine if weaker could effect the cure. The more rusty the iron is, the oftener we put it into the fire to purify it; and the more crooked it is, the more blows and the harder blows, we give to straighten it; therefore, Christian, if thou hast long been gathering rust, thou hast no cause to complain if God deal thus with thee.

All the chastening in the world, without divine teaching, will never make a man blessed. That man who finds correction attended with instruction, and lashing with lessoning, is a happy man.

When God's strokes and a Christian's strength are suited one to another, all is in love; let the load be ever so heavy that God lays on, if he put under his everlasting arms, all must be well.

Luther says, "If I might have my desire, I would rather choose the meanest work of a poor Christian, than all the victories and triumphs of Alexander or Julius Cæsar."

The best way to do ourselves good is to be doing good to others; the best way to gather is to scatter.

Many a man has slain his mercies, by setting too great a value upon them. Over-loved mercies are seldom long-lived mercies. The way to lose your mercies, is to indulge them; the way to destroy them is to fix your minds and hearts upon them.

As Joseph's heart was full of love to his brethren, even when he spake roughly to them and withdrew himself from them, for he was fain to go aside and ease his heart by weeping; so the heart of God is full of love to his people, even when he seems to be most displeased with them, and to turn his back upon them.

Such souls as have once been in the arms of God, in the midst of all oppositions, are as men made all of fire, walking in stubble; they consume and overcome all hindrances; all difficulties are but as whetstones to their fortitude. The moon will run her course, though the dogs bark at her; so will all those choice souls who have found warmth under Christ's wings run their Christian race in spite of all difficulties and danger.

Get this world, this moon, under your feet. Take no rest till you have broken through the silken net, till you have got off the golden fetters. A heart that is full of the world, is a heart full of wants.

The more we remember our days, the fewer
sins we shall have to number.

Though true repentance be never too late, yet
late repentance is seldom true.

Murmuring is a black garment, and it becomes
none so ill as saints.

Titus Vespasian never dismissed any petitioner
with a tear in his eye, or with a heavy heart;
and shall we think that the God of compassions
will always dismiss the petitioners of heaven
with tears in their eyes?   Surely no.

Faith is the key that unlocks Paradise and lets
a flood of joy into the soul.   Faith appropriates
all to itself.

They are rare Christians, indeed, who hold
their goodness and grow in goodness where
wickedness sits on the throne.   To be wheat
among tares, corn among chaff, pearls among
cockles, and roses among thorns, is truly excellent.

God will make the most insensible sinner sensible either of his hand here, or of his wrath in hell.

As all lights can not make up the want of the light of the sun, so all temporal comforts can not make up the want of one spiritual comfort.

Despairing thoughts make a man fight against God with his own weapons; they make a man cast all the cordials of the Spirit against the wall, as things of no value; they make a man suck poison out of the sweetest promises; they make a man eminent in nothing, unless it be in having hard thoughts of God, in arguing against his own soul and happiness, and in turning his greatest advantages into disadvantages, his greatest helps into his greatest hindrances.

Afflictions are evils in themselves, and we may desire and endeavor to be delivered from them. When Providence opens a door of escape, there is no reason why the saints should set themselves as marks and butts for their enemies to shoot at.

Assurance is glory in the bud; it is the suburbs of Paradise; it is a cluster of the land of promise; it is a spark of God; it is the joy and crown of a Christian; how great, therefore, is their impiety and folly who deny assurance, or who cry it down, under any names or notions whatsoever!

It is in vain for the bird to complain that it saw the corn, but not the pit-fall. So it will be vain for sinners to plead company and allurements, by which they have been enticed to undo their souls for ever. The God of spirits, the God of all flesh will not be put off with any excuses or pretenses when he shall try and judge the children of men.

When rich mercy and glorious power are nearest the soul, then Satan most storms and rages against the soul. The more the bowels of Christ work toward a sinner, the more furious will Satan assault that sinner.

Do not put off God to old age; for old, lame and sick sacrifices rarely reach as high as heaven.

8

Christians, remember this: God has two strings to his bow; if your hearts will not lie humble and low under the sense of sin and misery, he will make them lie low under the want of some desired mercy.

Affliction abases the loveliness of the world without that might entice us; it abates the lustfulness of the flesh within, which might else ensnare us; and it abates the spirit in his quarrel against the flesh and the world; by all which it proves a mighty advantage to us.

The more vile Christ made himself for us, the more dear he ought to be unto us.

The soul shall hear good news from heaven when it is waiting at wisdom's door.

God oftentimes delays, that his people may come to him with greater strength and importunity; he puts them off, that they may put on with more life and vigor. God seems to be cold, that he may make us the more hot; he seems to be slack, that he may make us the more earnest; he seems to be backward, that he may make us the more forward in pressing upon him.

A gracious soul has always his sins before his face; therefore, no wonder if the Lord casts them behind his back. The father soon forgets and casts behind his back those faults that the child remembers and has always in his eyes; so does the Father of spirits.

They say that nothing will dissolve the adamant but the blood of a goat; ah! nothing will kindly, sweetly and effectually break the hardened heart of a sinner but faith's beholding the blood of Christ trickling down his sides.

As many a man loses the sight of a city when he comes near to it, so many a choice soul loses the sight of heaven, even when it is nearest to heaven.

A little grace will put a man upon those religious duties that are easy and pleasing to flesh and blood, and not chargeable, but rather profitable and pleasurable; but it must be the *strength* of grace that puts a man upon those services that are costly and cross to the flesh.

Thou mayest write bitterness and death upon that mercy which has taken away thy heart from God.

That love which accompanies salvation is like the sun. The sun casts his beams upward and downward, to the east and to the west, to the north and to the south; so the love of a saint ascends to God above, and descends to men on earth; to our friends on the right hand, to our enemies on the left hand; to them that are in a state of grace, and to them that are in a state of nature. Divine love will still be working one way or another.

There is nothing that God is so tender of as he is of his glory; and nothing that his heart is so much set upon as his glory; and therefore he will vist his suffering people in a prison, and feast them in a dungeon, and walk with them in a fiery furnace, and show kindness to them in a lion's den; that every one may shout and cry, " Grace ! grace !"

It was a sweet saying of one, " As what I have, if offered to thee, pleaseth thee not, O Lord, without myself, so the good things we have from thee, though they may refresh us, yet they can not satisfy us without thyself."

Young saints often prove old angels, but old sinners seldom prove good saints.

Conflicts with Satan are usually the sharpest and hottest ; they spend and waste most the vital and noble spirit of the saints ; and therefore the Lord, after such conflicts, ordinarily gives his people his choicest and his strongest cordials.

As a sight of God's grace cheers the soul, so a sight of his greatness and glory silences the soul.

The sweetest comforts of this life are but like treasures of snow ; do but take a handful of snow and crush it in your hands, and it will melt away presently ; but if you let it lie upon the ground, it will continue for some time ; and

8*

so it is with the contentments of this world. If you grasp them in your hands, and lay them too near your heart, they will quickly melt and vanish away; but if you will not hold them too fast in your hands, nor lay them too close to your hearts, they will abide the longer with you.

Waiting souls, remember this: assurance is yours, but the time of giving it is the Lord's; the jewel is yours, but the season in which he will give it is in his own hand; the golden chain is yours, but he only knows the hour wherein he will put it around your necks. Well, wait patiently and quietly, wait expectingly and believingly, wait affectionately and wait diligently, and you shall find that Scripture made good with power upon your souls: "*Yet a little while, and he that shall come will come, and will not tarry*" (Hebrews, x. 17).

The mercies of God are not styled the *swift*, but *the sure mercies of David;* and, therefore, a gracious soul patiently waits for them.

All the acts and attributes of God sit at the feet of mercy. The weapons of God's artillery are turned into the rainbow; a bow indeed, but without an arrow; bent, but without a string.

Give God the cream and flower of youth, strength, time and talents. Vessels that are seasoned betimes with the savor of life never lose it.

What use would there be of the stars if the sun did always shine? why, none; and no more use would there be of your graces if assurance should be always continued.

God knows right well that if his left hand, in suffering times, be not under his people, and his right hand over them—if he do not give them some sips of sweetness, some relishes of goodness, they will quickly grow impatient and inconstant. But the smiles of God, the gracious discoveries of God, make their patience and constancy invincible.

Wine was the nearest when the watering pots were filled with water up to the brim; so oftentimes mercy is nearest, deliverance is nearest, when our afflictions are at the highest.

"Time," says Bernard, "were a good commodity in hell, and the traffic of it most gainful, where for one day a man would give ten thousand worlds, if he had them. Can we in good earnest believe this, and yet "*neglect so great salvation ?*"

Many a Christian has been made worse by the good things of this world; but where is the Christian that has been bettered by them?

Silence in afflictions is a Christian's armor of proof; it is that shield which no spear or dart of temptation can pierce. While a Christian lies quiet under the rod, he is safe. Satan may tempt him, but he will not conquer him; he may assault him, but he can not vanquish him.

God thrusts many a sharp spear through many a sinner's heart, and yet he feels nothing, he complains of nothing; these men's souls will bleed to death.

Cold prayers shall never have any warm answers. God will suit his returns to our requests;

Lifeless services shall have lifeless answers. When men are dull, God will be dumb.

The nature of a seal is to make things sure and firm among men; so the supper of the Lord is Christ's broad seal; it is his privy seal whereby he seals and assures his people that they are happy here—that they shall be more happy hereafter—that they are everlastingly beloved of their God; and that nothing shall be able to separate them from him who is their light, their life, their crown, their all in all.

Satan promises the best, but pays with the worst; he promises honor, and pays with disgrace; he promises pleasure, and pays with pain; he promises profit, and pays with loss; he promises life, and pays with death. But God pays as he promises; all his payments are made in pure gold.

Faith is a root grace, from whence spring all the sweet flowers of joy and peace. Faith is like the bee; it will suck sweetness out of every flower; it will extract light out of darkness, comforts out of distresses, mercies out of miseries, wine out of water, honey out of the rock, and meat out of the eater.

Afflictions are the saint's diet-drink; and where do you read in all the Scripture, that any of the saints ever drank of this diet-drink, and were not sensible of it?

Christian, thou must not neglect thy work, though God delay thy comfort; thou must be as obedient in the want of assurance, as thou art thankful under the enjoyment of assurance.

Reason's arm is too short to reach the jewel of assurance. This pearl of price is put into no. hand but that hand of faith that reaches from earth to heaven.

As green wood and old logs meet in one fire, so young sinners and old sinners meet in one hell and burn together.

That is not worthy the name of an affliction which does not strike at some bosom mercy; that trouble is no trouble which does not touch some choice contentment; that storm is no storm which only blows off the leaves, but never hurts the fruit; neither is that affliction any affliction which only reaches some remote enjoyment, but touches not a Joseph or a Benjamin.

It is not always high water with the saints sometimes they are reduced to a very low ebb. The best of saints are like the ark tossed up and down with waves, with fears, and doubts; and so it will be till they are quiet in the bosom of Christ.

Man's holiness is now his greatest happiness, and in heaven, man's greatest happiness will be his perfect holiness.

Seneca well says, that "though death is before the old man's face, yet he may be as near the young man's back." Man's life is the shadow of smoke, the dream of a shadow. One doubts whether to call it a dying life, or a living death.

God sometimes denies assurance to his dearest ones, at least for a time, that they may be kept humble and low in their own eyes. As the enjoyment of mercy gladdens us, so the want of mercy humbles us.

It is mercy to want mercy, till we are fit for mercy, till we are able to bear the weight of mercy, and make a divine improvement of mercy.

It is the very drift and design of the whole Scripture to bring souls first to an acquaintance *with* Christ, and then to an acceptance *of* Christ, and then to build them up in a sweet assurance of their actual interest in Christ.

He does well, that discourses of Christ; but he does infinitely better, that by experimental knowledge, feeds and lives on Christ.

Satan's great design is eternally to ruin souls; and where he can not do that, there he will endeavor to discomfit souls by busying them about the secret decrees and counsels of God, or by engaging them in such debates and disputes as neither men nor angels can certainly and infallibly determine, that so he may spoil their comforts, when he can not take away their crown.

Christ will be all in all, or he will be nothing at all. Though his coat was once divided, yet he will never suffer his crown to be divided.

Neglect of your graces is the ground of their decrease. Wells are the sweeter for drawing; you get nothing by dead and useless habits.

God loves to lade the wings of prayer with the choicest and chiefest blessings. Many Christians have found, by experience, praying times to be sealing times. They have found prayer to be a shelter to their souls, a sacrifice to God, a sweet savor to Christ, a scourge to Satan, and an inlet to assurance.

He that wants love to his brethren, wants one of the sweetest springs from whence assurance flows. A greater hell I would not wish any man, than to live and not to love the beloved of God.

Man's blood is apt to rise with his outward good. In the winter men gird their clothes closely about them, but in the summer they let them hang loose; in the winter of adversity

9

many a Christian girds his heart closely to God, to Christ, to the Gospel, to godliness, to ordinances, to duties, who, in the summer of mercy hangs loose from all.

The sight of God in an affliction is of irresistible efficacy to silence the heart, and to stop the mouth of a gracious man.

Faith has two hands, and with both she lays earnest and fast hold on king Jesus. Christ's beauty and glory are very taking and drawing; faith can not see them, but it will lay hold on them.

Souls at their first conversion are but roughcast, but God, by visiting them and manifesting himself to them in his ways, more and more fits them as vessels of mercy for glory.

Though the *salvation* of believers does not depend upon their knowledge of God being their Father, yet their *consolation* does: therefore, the Lord will not only be a Father to Israel, but he will make Israel know that he is his Father.

"Wilt thou not from this time cry unto me, My
Father, thou art the guide of my youth ?"

I have read of a very strange speech that
dropped from the lips of Epictetus, a heathen.
"If it be thy will," says he, "O Lord, command
me what thou wilt, send me whither thou wilt;
I will not withdraw myself from any thing that
seems good to thee." Ah! how will this heathen
rise in judgment at last against all those who are
partial in their obedience, who, while they yield
obedience to some commands, live in the habit-
ual breach of other commands!

There is no possibility of taking a mercy out
of God's hand, till the mercy be ripe for us, and
we ripe for the mercy.

The work of repentance is not the work of an
hour, a day, or a year, but the work of a life.
A sincere penitent makes as much conscience of
repenting daily, as he does of believing daily;
and he can as easily content himself with one act
of faith, or love, or joy, as he can content himself with one act of repentance.

A good heart will lie lowest when the hand of God is lifted highest. (Job, xlii. 1–6.)

Though there may be many precious gems and jewels in the house, yet the smoke may hinder a man from seeing them sparkle and shine: so, though there may be many precious graces in the souls of saints, yet corruptions may raise such a dust, such a smoke in the soul, that the soul is not able to see them in their beauty and glory. The well of water was near Hagar, but she saw it not till her eyes were opened by the Lord: so sometimes grace is near the soul, yea, in the soul, and yet the soul does not see it, till God opens the eye, and shows it.

There are those that love their mercies into their graves, that hug their mercies to death, that kiss them till they kill them. Many a man has slain his mercies by setting too great a value upon them. Over-loved mercies are seldom long-lived.

We may tempt God as well by neglecting means, as by trusting in means. It is best to use them, and in the use of them, to live above them.

Applicatory knowledge is the sweetest knowledge; it revives the heart, it cheers the spirits, it rejoices the soul; it makes a man go singing to duties, and go singing to his grave, and singing to heaven. Whereas others, though gracious, who want this appropriating knowledge, have their hearts full of fears, and their lives full of sorrows, and go sighing and mourning to heaven.

The lodestone can not draw iron when the diamond is in presence, no more can the beauties of this world draw the soul after them, when assurance, that choice pearl of price, is in presence.

No obedience but hearty obedience is acceptable to Christ; nothing takes Christ's heart but what comes from the heart.

Faith's putting Christ's righteousness on the soul, brings down blessings upon the soul. When Jacob had put on his elder brother's garment, he carried the blessing away.

9*

Faith will make a man endeavor to be good, yea, to be best at every thing he undertakes. It is not leaves, but fruit; not words, but works that God expects; and if we cross his expectation, we frustrate our own salvation, we further our own condemnation.

Oh, the precious time that is buried in the grave of murmuring! When the murmurer should be praying, he is murmuring against the Lord; when he should be hearing, he is murmuring against divine providences; when he should be reading, he is murmuring against instruments; and in these and a thousand other ways do murmurers expend that precious time which some would redeem with a world.

Grace does not destroy nature, but rather perfect it. Grace is of a noble offspring; it neither turns men into stocks nor into stoics.

Many a soul has surfeited of the world's dainties, and died for ever; but there is not a soul that has had the honor and happiness to be brought into Christ's banquetting house, and to eat and drink of his dainties, but it has lived for ever.

A gracious soul grieves more that God by his sin is grieved and dishonored, than he himself is afflicted and chastened for it.

Though Mary Magdalen was very near to Christ, yet she stands sighing, mourning, and complaining that they had stolen away her Lord, because she did not see him. Christians, though you may be very near and dear to Christ, yet till you come to see your assurance, you will spend you days in doubting, mourning, and complaining.

The *being* in a state of grace will yield a man a heaven hereafter, but the *seeing* of himself in this state will yield him both a heaven here and a heaven hereafter; it will render him doubly blest—blest in heaven, and blest in his own conscience.

Clothes and *company* do oftentimes tell tales in a mute but significant language.

Satan is such a grand enemy to the joy and peace, to the salvation and consolation of the saints, that he can not but make use of all his devices and stratagems to amaze and amuse, to disturb and disquiet the peace and rest of their souls. No sooner had Jesus Christ heard that lovely voice from heaven, " *This is my beloved Son, in whom I am well pleased,*" than he is desperately assaulted by Satan in the wilderness. No sooner was Paul dropped out of heaven, after he had seen such visions of glory as were unutterable, than he was presently set upon and buffeted by Satan.

He that makes God the *object* of prayer, but not the *end* of prayer; does but lose his prayer, and take pains to undo himself. The end must always be as noble as the means, or else a Christian acts below himself, yea, below his very reason.

Other sins will not be long-lived when justice is done upon the bosom sin. Thrust but a dart through the heart of Absalom, and a complete conquest will follow.

Grace and glory differ very little; the one is the seed, the other is the flower; grace is glory militant, glory is grace triumphant; and a man may as well plead for equal degrees of grace in this world, as he may plead for equal degrees of glory in another world.

Those two lovers, grace and assurance, are not by God so nearly joined together but that they may, by sin on our side and justice on God's, be put asunder.

There is a mighty difference between the workings of the Spirit and the witness of the Spirit. There are oftentimes many glorious and efficacious works of the Spirit, as faith, love, repentance, holiness, where there is not the witness of the Spirit. David had the Spirit, and many sweet workings of the Spirit in him and upon him at the very time when he had by sin lost the witness and testimony of the spirit. (Psalm li. 10–12).

Faith makes a man see the prickles that are in every rose, the thorns that are in every crown, the poison that is in the golden cup, the spot that is in the shining pearl; and thus a Christian counts and calls all these things, as indeed they are, "*vanity of vanities.*"

Christ went to heaven in a cloud, and the angel went up to heaven in the smoke and flame of the sacrifice; so doubtless do many precious souls ascend to heaven in clouds and darkness.

After much praying, waiting and weeping, God usually comes with his hands and his heart full of mercy to his people. He loves not to come empty-handed to those who have sat long with tearful eyes at mercy's door.

There is no water so sweet as the saint's tears, when they do not overflow the banks of moderation. Tears are not mutes; they have a voice, and their oratory is of great prevalency with the Almighty God.

Hope, exercised upon the promise, brings heaven down to the heart. The promise is the same to hope that hope is to the soul; the promise is the anchor of hope, as hope is the anchor of the soul.

Divine knowledge fills. a man with spiritual activity. It will make a man work, as if he would be saved by his work; and yet it will make a man believe that he is saved only upon the account of free grace.

Temptations make a Christian more serviceable and useful to others. None so fit and able to relieve tempted souls, to sympathize with tempted souls, to succor tempted souls, to counsel tempted souls, to pity tempted souls, to bear with tempted souls, and to comfort tempted souls as those who have been in the school of temptation.

Soul opportunities are worth more than a thousand worlds. Mercy is in them, grace and glory are in them, heaven and eternity are in them.

Cold prayers are as arrows without heads, as swords without edges, as birds without wings; they pierce not, they cut not, they fly not up to heaven. Cold prayers always freeze before they reach heaven.

A well-grounded assurance is always attended with three fair handmaids: love, humility and holy joy.

God regards not so much the matter as the manner of our prayer. God loves adverbs better than nouns; not praying only, but praying well; not doing good, but doing it well.

A sincere heart weeps and laments bitterly over those secret and inward corruptions, which others will scarcely acknowledge to be sins.

A sullen silence is both a sin and a punishment. There is a generation among us who, when they are under the afflicting hand of God, have no mouths to plead with God, no lips to praise God, no tongues to justify God; these are possessed with a dumb devil; they wrong many at once, God and Christ, bodies and souls.

There is not the lowest good that is below the humble soul. If the work be good, though never so low, humility will put a hand to it; so will not pride.

Divine knowledge is the beginning of eternal life; it is a spark of glory; it works life in the soul; it is a taste and pledge of eternal life.

God often delays the giving of assurance, not because he delights to keep his children in fears and doubts, nor because he thinks assurance is too rare, too great, too choice a jewel to bestow upon them; but it is either because he thinks their souls are so taken up and filled with creature enjoyments as that Christ is put to lodge in an outhouse; or else it is because they pursue not after assurance with all their might; they give not all *diligence to make their calling and election sure ;* or else it is because their hearts are not prepared, are not *low* enough for so *high* a favor.

He that will not break the hedge of a fair command to avoid the foul way of some heavy affliction, may well conclude that his affliction is in love.

Christians, your hearts are Christ's royal throne, and in this throne Christ will be chief. If you shall attempt to throne the creature, be it never so near and dear unto you, Christ will dethrone it, he will destroy it. He will quickly lay them in a bed of dust who shall aspire to his royal throne.

Perseverance is not a particular distinct grace of itself, but such a virtue as crowns all virtue; it is such a grace as casts a general beauty and glory upon every grace; it is a grace that leads every grace on to perfection.

As he can not be wise who speaks much, so he can not be known for a fool who says nothing. There are many wise fools in the world. There are many silly souls who, by holding their tongues, gain the credit and honor of being discreet men. Silence is so rare a virtue where wisdom regulates it, that it is accounted a virtue where folly imposes it.

Where Christ has set his name, there, Christian, set thou thine heart. Call things as Christ calls them; count things as Christ counts them; that should not be little in thine eye which is great in the eye of Christ; nor should that be

great in thine eye which is but little in the eye
of Christ.

King Antigonus pulling a sheep with his own
hands out of a dirty ditch, as he was passing by,
drew his subjects exceedingly to commend and
love him. So King Jesus, pulling poor souls
out of their sins—and, as it were, out of hell—
can not but draw them to be much in the com-
mendation of Christ, and strong in their love to
Christ.

Were there more assurance among Christians,
they would not count great mercies small mercies, and small mercies no mercies; no; then
every mercy on this side hell would be a great
mercy, then every mercy would be a sweeter
mercy, a perfumed mercy.

Christ does not measure his gifts by our peti-
tions, but by his own riches and mercy. Gracious souls many times receive gifts and favors
from God that they never dreamed of nor durst
presume to ask. Jesus Christ is often better
than his word.

Happiness lies not in any transient act of the Spirit, as assurance is, but in the more permanent and lasting acts of the Spirit. If a man's eternal happiness *did* lie in the assurance of his happiness, then might a man be crowned with the steersman of Xerxes in the morning, and be beheaded with him in the evening of the same day.

The least sin is rather to be avoided and prevented than the greatest sufferings. If this cockatrice be not crushed in the egg it will soon become a serpent; the very thought of sin, if but thought on, will break forth into action, action into custom, custom into habit, and then both body and soul are lost irrecoverably to all eternity.

No action, no service goes current in heaven but that which is sealed up with integrity of heart. God will not be put off with the shell when we give the devil the kernel.

Woe, woe to the soul that fights against God with his own mercies; that will be sinful, because he is merciful. Abused mercy will at last turn into a lion, a fierce lion, and then woe to the despisers and abusers of it!

The richest metals lie lowest, the choicest gems are in the bowels of the earth, and they who will have them must search diligently and dig deep, or else they must go without them. Doubting souls, you must search and dig again and again, and you must work and labor, if ever you will find those spiritual treasures, those pearls of price, that are hid under the ashes of corruption, that lie low in the very bowels of your souls.

Spiritual hungerings and thirstings are satisfied only with spiritual things. "*Show us the father, and it sufficeth us*" (John xiv. 8). All things in the world can not suffice us, but a sight of the father will satisfy us.

God never has and never will fail the waiting soul. Though God loves to try the patience of his children, yet he does not love to tire out the patience of his children; therefore he will not contend for ever, neither will he be always wroth, lest the spirits of his people should fail.

Christian, if thou art dear to God, God will, by striking thy dearest mercy, put thee upon striking at thy darling sin; therefore hold thy peace, even when God touches the apple of thine eye.

As our greatest good comes through the sufferings of Christ, so God's greatest glory that he hath from his saints comes through their sufferings.

Sincerity is the very queen of virtues; she holds the throne, and will be sure to keep it. Yea, the very sight of it in the soul makes a man sit cheerful and thankful. Noah-like in the midst of all tempests and storms.

A gracious soul knows that if he is rich in faith he can not be poor in other graces; he knows the growth of faith will be as the former and latter rain to all other graces; he knows that there is no way to outgrow his fears but by growing in faith; therefore his cry is, "O Lord, whatever I am weak in, let me be strong in *faith;* whatever dies, let *faith* live; whatever decays, let *faith* flourish.

Three things a Christian should steadily labor to maintain: the honor of God, the honor of the Gospel and the honor of his own name. If once a Christian's good name sets in a cloud, it will be long before it rises again.

When God gives a mercy, he does not relinquish his own right in that mercy.

Believer, it may be thou art not yet fit for so choice a mercy as assurance ; thou art not able to bear so great a favor. Many heads are not able to bear strong waters. The very quintessence of all the strong consolations of God are wrung out into the golden cup of assurance; could you drink of this cup and not stagger?

A holy silence allays all tumults in the mind, and makes a man in patience to possess his own soul, which, next to his possession of God, is the choicest and sweetest possession in all the world.

Assurance is the top and beauty of a Christian's glory in this life. It is usually attended with the strongest joy, with the sweetest comforts, and with the greatest peace. But alas! alas!

it is a pearl that most want, a crown that few wear.

Christ is the pot of manna, the cruise of oil, a bottomless ocean of all comfort, content and satisfaction. He that has him, wants nothing. He that wants him, enjoys nothing.

God often gives assurance in one ordinance, when he denies it in another, that we may seek his face in all. God loves as well that we should *wait* on him, as that we should *wrestle* with him.

Long afflictions will much set off the glory of heaven. The longer the storm, the sweeter the calm; the longer the winter nights, the sweeter the summer days. The new wine of Christ's kingdom is most sweet to those who have long been drinking gall and vinegar. The higher the mountain, the gladder we shall be when we get to the top of it. The longer our journey is, the sweeter will be our end; and the longer our passage is, the more desirable will the haven be.

There is no sickness so little, but God has a finger in it, though it be but the aching of the little finger. As the scribe is more eyed and more properly said to write than the pen; and as every workman is more eyed and more properly said to effect his works, than the tools which he uses as his instruments—so the Lord, who has the greatest hand in all our afflictions, is far more to be eyed and owned than any inferior or subordinate causes whatever.

Justice always makes mercy dumb, when sin has made the sinner deaf.

Many there are whose love to the saints is like Job's brooks, which in winter, when we have no need, overflow with tenders of service and shows of love; but when the season is hot and dry, and the poor thirsty traveler stands in most need of water to refresh him, then the brooks are quite dried up. But such as *truly* love, will *always* love.

A murmurer is an ungodly man: he is an ungodlike man; no man on earth more unlike to God than the murmurer; and therefore no wonder if, when Christ comes to execute judgment, he deals severely and terribly with him. Let

him make what profession he will of godliness ;
yet if murmuring keeps the throne in his heart,
Christ will deal with him at last as with ungodly
sinners.

A lazy Christian will always want four things
—comfort, content, confidence, and assurance.
Assurance and joy are choice donatives that
Christ gives to laborious Christians only. The
lazy Christian has his mouth full of complaints,
when the active Christian has his heart full of
comforts.

Austin, upon that answer of God to Moses,
" *Thou canst not see my face and live*," makes this
quick and sweet reply, " Then, Lord, let me die,
that I may see thy face."

God loves to smile most upon his people, when
the world frowns most. When the world puts
its iron chains upon their legs, then God puts his
golden chains about their necks; when the world
puts a bitter cup into their hands, then God drops
some of his honey, some of his goodness and
sweetness, into it. When the world is ready to
stone them, then God gives them the white

stone; and when the world is tearing their good names, then he gives them a new name, that none knows but he that has it, a name that is better than that of sons and daughters.

Men who content themselves with negative righteousness, shall find at last heaven's gates bolted upon them with a double bolt. All that negative righteousness and holiness can do, is to help a man to one of the best chambers and easiest beds in hell.

Never complain that thy afflictions are greater than others', except thou canst evidence that thy sins are less than others'.

Remember it is dangerous to yield to the least sin, in order to be rid of the greatest temptation. The least sin set home upon the conscience, will more wound, vex, and oppress the soul, than all the temptations in the world can do.

Knowledge and love, like the water and the ice, beget each other. Man loves Christ by knowing, and knows Christ by loving.

Christian, shall the counterfeit gold that is in the world make men active and diligent to get that which is current, and which will abide the touch-stone and the fire ; and shall not that counterfeit assurance which is in the world provoke your heart to be so much the more careful and active to get such a well-grounded assurance as God accounts current, as will abide his touchstone in the day of discovery, and as will keep a man from shame and blushing, when the throne shall be set, and the books shall be opened ?

The bee stores her hive out of all sorts of flowers for the common benefit; so a heavenly Christian sucks sweetness out of every mercy and every duty, out of every providence and every ordinance, out of every promise and every privilege, that he may give out the more sweet-ness to others.

No man can paint the sweetness of the honey-comb, the sweetness of a cluster of Canaan, the sweetness of paradise, the fragrancy of the rose of Sharon. As the being of things can not be painted, and as the sweetness of things can not be painted, no more can that assurance and joy,

that flow from believing, be painted or expressed; they are too great and too glorious for weak
man to picture or set forth.

Where Christ loves, he always begets a love
something like his own. That love which is flat,
lukewarm, or cold, will leave a man to freeze on
this side heaven: yea, it will fit him for the
warmest place in hell.

Ah! souls—if your knowledge does not put
the world under your feet, it will never put a
crown of glory upon your heads. The church
that is clothed with the sun, and has a crown of
stars upon her head, has the moon under her
feet. (Revelations, xii. 1.)

Noah's sacrifice could not be great, and yet it
was greatly accepted and highly accounted of by
God. Such is God's condescending love to weak
worms, that he looks more at their will than at
their work; he minds more what they would do,
than what they do; he always prefers the willing mind before the worthiest work; and where
desires and endeavors are sincere, there God

11

judges such to be as good as they desire and endeavor to be.

Love cares not what it is nor what it does, so that it may but advance the Lord Jesus. It makes the soul willing to be a footstool for Christ; to be any thing, to be nothing, that Christ may be all in all.

Believer, by living without assurance, you lay yourself open to all Satan's snares and temptations; yea, you instigate and provoke Satan to tempt you to the worst of sins, to tempt you to the greatest neglects, to tempt you to the strangest shifts, and to reduce you to the saddest straits. Ah, Christian, in what has Satan so gratified you, that you should thus gratify him?

No man honors God, and no man justifies God at so high a rate, as he who lays his hand upon his mouth, when the rod of God is upon his back.

The world, by the glistening of her pomp and preferment, has slain millions; like the serpent Scytale, who, when she can not overtake the fleeing passengers, does, with her beautiful colors, astonish and amaze them so that they have no power to pass away till she has stung them to death. Adversity has slain her thousands, but prosperity her tens of thousands.

Among the philosophers there were two hundred and eighty opinions concerning happiness, some affirming happiness to lie in one thing, some in another; but by the Spirit and the Word we are taught that happiness lies in our oneness with God, in our nearness and dearness to God, and in our conformity to God. Mark, the Scripture pronounces him happy, whose hope is in God, though he want assurance. *Happy is he that hath the God of Jacob for his help, whose hope is in the Lord his God.* (Psalm cxlvi. 5.)

In the law, God called for the first of all things; he required not only the first fruits, but the very first of the first (Exodus, xxiii. 19); and in Leviticus, ii. 14, he is so passionately set upon having the first of the first, that he will not stay till the ears of corn are ripe, but will have the green ears dried in the fire. And what

would God teach us by all this, but to serve him
with the first fruits of our age, the morning of
our youth?

Ah, souls, while you are in the very service
of the Lord, you will find by experience that the
God of heaven will prosper you, and support
you, and encourage and strengthen you, and
carry you through the hardest service with the
greatest sweetness and cheerfulness that can be.
He will suit your strength to your work, and in
the hardest service you will have the choicest
assistance.

In the Old Testament, the Jews being babes
and infants in grace and holiness, had a world
of temporal promises, and very few spiritual
ones; but now in the days of the Gospel the
Lord is pleased to double and treble his Spirit
upon his people, and we meet with very few
temporal promises in the Gospel, it is full of
spiritual blessings.

Idleness is the very source of sin. Standing
pools gather mud, and nourish and breed venom-

ous creatures; and so do the hearts of idle and slothful Christians.

Believer, thy afflictions are not to be compared to those that attended our Lord Jesus, whose whole life, from the cradle to the cross, was nothing but a life of suffering. Osorius, writing of the sufferings of Christ, says, that the crown of thorns bored his head with seventy-two wounds. Many seventy-two afflictions did Christ meet with whilst he was in this world; he was *a man of sorrows* and *acquainted* with grief. A man might as well compare the number of his bosom friends with the stars in heaven, as compare his afflictions with the sufferings of Christ.

When God teaches thy reins as well as thy brains, thy heart as well as thy head, these lessons are all in love.

A proud heart eyes more his seeming worth, than his real want. But a soul truly humbled blushes to see his own righteousness, and glories in this, that he has the righteousness of Christ to live upon.

11*

The Spirit of the Lord will not suffer his choicest jewel, *grace*, to be always buried under the straw and stubble of parts and gifts.

There is nothing that God is so tender of as he is of his glory, and nothing that his heart is so much set upon as his glory; therefore will he visit his children in a prison, and feast them in a dungeon, and walk with them in a fiery furnace, and show kindness to them in a lion's den; that every one may shout and cry, "Grace, grace."

The most dangerous vermin are too often to be found under the fairest and sweetest flowers; and the fairest glove is often drawn upon the foulest hand, and the richest robes are often put upon the most diseased bodies; so are the fairest and sweetest names upon the greatest and most horrible vices and errors that are in the world. Oh, that we had not so many sad proofs of this among us.

It is not in the power of any mortal to repent at pleasure. Some ignorant deluded souls vainly conceive that these five words, "Lord, have

mercy upon me," are efficacious to send them
to heaven ; but as many are undone by buying
a counterfeit jewel, so many are in hell by mis·
take of their repentance ; many rest in their repentance though it be but the shadow and not
the substance ; which caused one to say, " Repentance damneth more than sin."

Humility fits for the highest services we owe
to Christ, and yet will not neglect the lowest
service to the meanest saint.   Humility can feed
upon the meanest dish, and yet it is maintained
by the choicest delicacies, as God, Christ and
glory.

That sorrow for sin which keeps the soul from
looking toward the mercy seat, and which keeps
Christ and the soul asunder, or which renders
the soul unfit for the communion of saints, is a
sinful sorrow.

The strongest faith is subject at times to
shakings, as the stoutest ships are to tossings,
as the wisest men are to doubtings, as the bright-
est stars are to twinklings.   Therefore, Christian, if at certain times thou shouldest not be

sensible of the growth of thy faith, yet do not conclude that thou hast no faith. Faith may be in the habit when it is not in the act; there may be life in the root of the tree when there are neither leaves, blossoms nor fruit upon the tree ; but they will show themselves in the spring, and so will the habits of faith break forth into acts when the Sun of righteousness shall shine forth, and make it a pleasant spring to the soul.

Faith engages *God* in every encounter, and who can stand before a consuming fire? Mary, Queen of Scots, mother to King James, was wont to say that she feared Master Knox's prayers, who was a man of much faith, more than an army of ten thousand men.

The soul is never able to stand under the guilt and weight of the least sin when God sets it home upon the soul. The least sin will press and sink the stoutest sinner as low as hell when God shall open the sinner's eyes and make him see the horrid filthiness and abominable vileness that are in sin.

The devil counts a fit occasion half a conquest,

for he knows that corrupt nature has a seed-plot for all sin, which being drawn forth and watered by some sinful occasion, is soon set awork to the producing of death and destruction. God will not remove the temptation till we remove the occasion.

Ah, souls, till you are taken up into the bosom of Christ your comforts will not be full, pure and constant; till then, Satan will still be thwarting you and spreading snares to entangle you ; therefore you should always be crying out with the Church, *Come, Lord Jesus.*

The Lord has in the Scripture discovered the several snares, plots and devices that the devil has to undo the souls of men ; that so being forewarned they may be forearmed; that they may be always upon their watch tower, and hold their weapons in their hands, as the Jews did in Nehemiah's time.

When a man has been in heaven as many millions of years as there are stars in heaven, his glory shall be as fresh and as green as it was at his first entrance there. All worldly glory is like the flowers of the field, but the glory that Christ gives is lasting and durable like himself.

Divine favor is, as it were, a jewel locked up; but by finding Christ, by getting Christ, the soul gets this jewel that is more worth than a world; yea, by gaining him, the soul gains *lives;* to wit, a life of grace and a life of glory; and what would the soul have more?

We see, by woeful experience, Christ neglected, despised, scorned and trampled upon by most; and no wonder, for many preach themselves more than Christ, and their own notions and impressions more than Christ. Surely Christ is little beholden to such ministers, and, I think, the souls of men as little. Oh, that they were so wise as to consider of it and lay it to heart! For surely a real Christian cares not for any thing that has not something of Christ in it

Souls rich in grace practice that themselves which they prescribe to others.

Should God chain up Satan, and give him no liberty to tempt or entice the sons of men to vanity or folly, yet they would not, they could not but sin against him by reason of that cursed nature that is in them, which will still be provoking them to those sins which stir up the anger of God against them.

A man full of hope will be full of action; a lively hope and a diligent hand are inseparable companions. Hope will make a man do, though he die for doing.

Oh, that the young would begin to be good betimes, that so they may have the greater harvest of joy when they come to be old! It is sad to be sowing seed when you should be reaping your harvest. It is best to gather the summer of youth against the winter of old age.

If thou wouldest be good betimes, then thou must acquaint thyself with *Jesus Christ* betimes. A man never begins to be good till he begins to know him who is the fountain of all goodness.

There are three things that earthly riches can never do; they can never satisfy divine justice, they can never pacify divine wrath, nor can they ever quiet a guilty conscience. And till these things are done man is undone.

Deliverance from Satan's snares carries with it the clearest and the greatest evidence of the soul and heart of God to be toward us. Many a man, by the common hand of Providence, escapes the snares that men lay for him, but yet escapes not the snares that Satan has laid for him. Such deliverances are fruits of special love.

Dissolution is the daughter of dissension. Oh, how does the name of Christ and the way of Christ suffer by discord of saints! How are many that are entering upon the ways of God, hindered and saddened, and the mouths of the wicked opened, and their hearts hardened against God and his ways by the discord of his people! Remember this : the disagreement of Christians is the devil's triumph ; and what a sad thing is this that Christians should give Satan cause to triumph !

Sin and punishment are linked together with chains of adamant.

Grace is a perpetually flowing fountain. It is compared to water, which serves to cool men when they are in a burning heat; so grace cools the soul when it has been even scorched and burnt up by the sense of Divine wrath and displeasure. Water is cleansing; so is grace. Water is fructifying; so is grace. And water is satisfying; it satisfies the thirsty, and so does grace. (John, iv. 13, 14.)

The least sin should humble the soul, but certainly the greatest sin should never discourage the soul, much less should it work the soul to despair. Despairing Judas perished, whereas the murderers of Christ, believing on him, were saved.

A man may not look intently upon that which he may not love entirely. It is best and safest to have the eye always fixed upon the highest and noblest objects, as the mariner's eye is fixed upon the star when his hand is upon the helm.

If vain thoughts, *resisted and lamented*, could stop the current of mercy and render a soul unhappy, there would be none on earth that would

ever taste of mercy or be everlastingly happy.
Such thoughts abhorred, resisted· and disclaimed,
are not sins upon our souls, though troubles to
our mind.

Reader, remember this: if thy knowledge do
not now affect thy heart, it will at last, with a
witness, afflict thy heart; if it do not now endear
Christ to thee, it will at last provoke Christ the
more against thee; if it do not make all the
things of Christ to be very precious in thy eyes,
it will at last make thee the more vile in Christ's
eyes.

It was a good saying of one, " God hears not
the words of one that prays unless he that prays
hears them first himself ;" and, verily, God will
never understand that prayer which we do not
understand ourselves. To pray in a right manner is to pray " *with the understanding.*"

Christians, make more care and conscience of
keeping up your peace with God. It is remiss-
ness herein which occasions much of that sour-
ness, bitterness and strife among you. You
have not, as you should, kept up your peace

with God, and therefore it is that you do so dreadfully break the peace among yourselves. The Lord has promised " *that when a man's ways please him, he will make his enemies to be at peace with him.*" Ah, how much more then would God make the children of peace to keep the peace among themselves if their ways did but please him.

He who lives up to a little light shall have more light; he who lives up to a little knowledge shall have more knowledge; he who lives up to a little faith shall have more faith, and he who lives up to a little love shall have more love. Verily the main reason why men are such babes and shrubs in grace is because they do not live up to their attainments.

Satan must have a double leave before he can do any thing against us. He must have his commission from God, and leave from ourselves, before he can act any thing against our happiness. When he tempts, we must assent; when he makes offers, we must hearken; when he commands, we must obey, or else all his labor and temptations will be frustrated; and the evil that he tempts us to shall be put down only to his account.

A watchful soul is a soul upon the wing, a soul out of gunshot, a soul upon a rock, a soul in a castle, a soul above the clouds, a soul held fast in everlasting arms.

He is a brave Christian, and has much of Christ within, who accounts nothing his own that he does not communicate to others. The bee stores her hive out of all sorts of flowers for the common benefit, and why then in this should not every Christian be like a bee?

It is much to be very gracious when a man is very great; and to be high in holiness, when advanced to high places. Usually, men's blood rises with their outward good. Certainly there are worthy ones, and shall walk with Christ in white, whose garments are not defiled with greatness or riches.

A humble soul judges himself to be below the wrath and judgment of God. He looks upon himself as one not worthy that God should spend a rod upon him in order to his reformation, edification, or salvation. He can not but count and call every thing a mercy that is less than hell. But proud hearts think themselves wronged when they are afflicted; and cry out with Cain, " *Our punishment is greater than we can bear.*"

A humble soul knows, that to bless God in prosperity, is the way to increase it; and to bless God in adversity, is the way to remove it.

Satan often paints sin with virtue's colors. He knows that if he should present it in its own nature and dress, the soul would rather fly from it, than yield to it, and therefore he presents it unto us, not in its own proper colors, but painted and gilded over with the name and show of virtue, that we may the more easily be overcome by it, and take the more pleasure in committing it.

The world gives, and then reproaches the recipient for receiving; but where Christ gives, he will not upbraid, neither with present failings nor former infirmities. He will always *rejoice over them to do them good.*

Let no knowledge satisfy thee, but that which lifts thee above the world, but that which weans thee from the world, but that which makes the world a footstool. *Such* knowledge, *such* light, will at last lead thee into everlasting light.

No way to honor God, no way to win souls, no way to increase your own gifts and graces, but to exercise them for the good of others. Grace is not like to worldly vanities, that diminish by distribution, but like candles, which keep the same light, though a thousand are lighted by them. Grace is like the widow's oil, which multiplied by pouring out; and like those talents which doubled by employment.

To venture upon the occasion of sin, and then to pray, *Lead us not into temptation*, is the same as to thrust thy finger into the fire, and then pray that it may not be burnt.

All our murmurings, which are so many arrows shot at God himself, will return upon our own heads; they reach not him, but they will hit us; they hurt not him, but they will wound us: it is better to be mute than to murmur—it is dangerous to provoke a consuming fire.

Aristotle requires this in an orator, that he be a good man. How much more then should God's orators be good and gracious? Unholy ministers pull down instead of building up. O the souls that their lives destroy! By their loose lives they lead their flocks to hell, where themselves must lie lowermost.

" *Whatsoever thy hand findeth to do, do it with all thy might*" (Ecclesiastes, ix. 10). Mark, the Scripture does not say, what thy *head* finds to do; that may find a thousand things: nor what thy *heart* finds to do, for that may find ten thousand things: but what *thy hand findeth to do;* that is, look what work God cuts out to thy hand to do; that do with all thy might, for there is no working in the grave. We are to do much good in a little time. Our time is short, our task is great.

There is the seed of all sins, of the vilest and worst of sins, in the best of men.

That which a Papist reports of their sacrament of the mass—" That there are as many mysteries in it as there are drops in the sea, dust on the earth, angels in the heavens, stars in the sky, atoms in the sunbeams, or sands on the sea-shore,"—may be truly asserted of the Word of God. No study equal to the study of the Scripture, for profit and comfort.

It was for those very sins that Satan paints and puts fine colors on, that the Creator was made a creature, that he who was clothed with glory was wrapped with rags of flesh, that the God of the law was subject to the law, the God of circumcision circumcised, that he who binds the devils in chains was tempted, the God of strength made weary, the Judge of all flesh condemned, the Lord of life put to death. O how should the consideration of this stir up the soul against sin, and work the soul to fly from it, and use all holy means whereby it may be subdued and destroyed!

Our hearts are the Spirit's harps. If a man should always touch one string in an instrument, he would never play various tunes, he would never make pleasant music; neither would the Spirit, if he should be always doing one thing in the soul; therefore he acts variously.

Be sure, Christian, you always reflect upon your graces, and whatsoever good is in you, with caution. Your graces are gifts of grace, favors given you from above, gifts dropped out of heaven into your heart, flowers plucked from the garden of Paradise. Keep humble, therefore: *what hast thou that thou hast not received?*

The tree grows downward, when it does not grow upward; so a soul may grow rich in some particular graces, when it does not thrive in others; it may grow rich in humility, in self-denial, in meekness, in temperance, when it does not grow up in joy, and delight, and comfort.

He who thinks he has enough of the *Holy Spirit*, will quickly find himself vanquished by the *evil* spirit.

Many men lose their comfort, as Saul lost his kingdom, by not discerning the time to be spiritually rich. The merchant will not lose his opportunity of buying, nor the sailor his of sailing, nor the husbandman of sowing; and why, Christian, should you lose yours of growing rich in grace?

Of all mercies, pardoning mercy is the most sweetening mercy. It is a mercy that makes all other mercies look like mercies, and taste like mercies, and work like mercies. He who has it can not be miserable; he who wants it, can not be happy.

As the peacock, looking upon his black feet, lets fall his plumes, so the poor soul, when he looks upon his black feet, the vanity of his mind, the body of sin, that is in him, his proud spirit falls low.

As weeds endanger the corn, as bad humors endanger the blood, or as an infected house endangers the neighborhood; so does the company of the bad endanger those that are good. Entireness with wicked consorts is one of the strongest chains of hell, and binds us to a participation of both sin and punishment.

It is not he who receives most of the truth into his *head*, but he who receives it affectionately into his *heart*, that shall enjoy the happiness of having his judgment sound and clear, when others shall be deluded and deceived by those who make it their business to infect the judgments and undo the souls of men.

Faith has a happy hand, and never but speeds in one kind or another. It has what it would, either in money or in money's worth. A believing husband, wife, child, or servant may bring down, by the actings of faith, many a blessing upon their relations.

Miseries always lie at that man's door who leans upon any thing below Christ: such a man is most in danger; and this is not his least plague, that he thinks himself secure.

Every man obeys Christ as he prizes Christ, and no otherwise. The higher price any soul sets upon Christ, the more noble will that soul be in its obedience to Christ.

Strong saints must not deal by the weak as the

herd of deer deal by the wounded deer; they forsake it and push it away. But when a poor weak saint is wounded by a temptation, or by the power of some corruption, then they that are strong ought to succor and support such an one, lest he be swallowed up of sorrow.

True repentance is a gift that is from above; and if the Lord does not give it, man will eternally perish for the want of it.

A saint should be like a seraph, beset all over with eyes and lights, that he may avoid Satan's snares, and stand fast in the hour of temptation.

Sinner, remember this—grievous is the torment of the damned for the bitterness of their punishment, but most grievous for the *eternity* of the punishment; for to be tormented without end, this is that which goes beyond the bounds of all description. O that you would repent and return, that your souls might live for ever!

Adversity abases the loveliness of the world, that might entice us; it abates the lustfulness of the flesh within, that might incite us to folly and vanity ; and it abets the spirit in its quarrel with the two former, which tends much to the reviving and recovering of decayed graces.

To repent of sin is as great a work of grace as not to sin.

Weak saint, when thou art fretful and desponding, think what would not a lost soul, that had been but an hour in hell, give for a drop of that grace thou hast in thy heart; think seriously of this, and be thankful.

Though no believer does what he should do, yet doubtless every believer might do more than he does, in order to God's glory, and his own and others' internal and external good. We have many promises concerning divine assistance; and if we did but stir up the grace of God that is in us, we should find the assistance of God, and the glorious breaking forth of his power and love, according to his promise and the work that he requires of us. They are blessed that do what they can, though they can not but under do.

13

Remember this—you will never be rich in grace if you care not *whom* you hear, nor *what* you hear.

It is not usual with God to leave his people frequently to relapse into enormities; for by his spirit and grace, by his smiles and frowns, by his word and rod, he usually preserves them from these; yet he does leave his choicest ones frequently to relapse into *infirmities* (and of his grace he pardons them in course), as idle words, passion, and vain thoughts. And though gracious souls strive against, complain of, and weep over these, yet the Lord, to keep them humble, leaves them oftentimes to such relapses; but they shall never be their bane, because they are their burden.

It is a just and righteous thing with God, that he should fall into the pit who will adventure to dance upon the brink thereof; and that he should be a slave to sin who will not flee from the occasions of sin. As long as there is fuel in our hearts for a temptation, we can not be secure. He who has gunpowder about him, had need keep far enough off from sparks.

Let but a Christian compare his external losses with his spiritual, internal and eternal gain, and he will find that for every penny that he loses in the service of God he gains a pound ; and for every pound that he loses he gains a hundred ; for every hundred lost he gains a thousand. We lose pins in his service, and find pearls ; we lose the favor of the creature, and peace with the creature, and we gain the favor of God, peace with conscience, and the comfort and contents of a better life.

If there were but one farthing of that debt unpaid which Christ was engaged to satisfy, it would not have been consistent with the unspotted justice of God to have let him come into heaven and sit down at his own right hand ; but all our debts by his death being discharged, we are free, and he is exalted to sit down at the right hand of his Father, which is the top of his glory, and the greatest pledge of our felicity.

Oh, how unlike to God are those preachers who think to correct the divine wisdom and eloquence with their own vanity, novelty and sophistry ! Jesus Christ himself, the great Doctor of the church, teacheth them a lesson on this point : *"And with many such parables spake he the word unto them, as they were able to hear it"* (Mark, iv. 33). Not as he was able to have spoken ; he could have expressed himself at a higher rate than any mortal can ; he could have soared to the clouds ; he knew how to knit such knots that they could never untie, but he would not ; he delighted to speak to his hearers' shallow capacities. *" I have yet many things to say unto you, but ye can not bear them now"* (John, xvi. 12).

Nothing humbles and breaks the heart of a sinner like mercy and love. Souls that converse much with sin and wrath, may be much terrified ; but souls that converse much with grace and mercy, will be much humbled.

Weak Christians are very apt to make sense and feeling the judge of their spiritual estate and condition ; and therefore, upon every turn, they count themselves miserable, and conclude that they have no grace because they can not feel it, nor discern it, nor believe it ; and so making sense, feeling and reason the judge of their estate, they wrong, and vex, and perplex their precious souls, as if it were not one thing *to be* the Lord's, and another thing for a man *to know that* he is the Lord's; as if it were not one thing for a man to have grace, and another thing to know that he has grace.

There is oftentimes a great deal of knowledge where there is but little wisdom to improve that knowledge. It is not the *most knowing* Christian, but the *most wise* Christian that sees, avoids and escapes Satan's snares. Knowledge without wisdom is like mettle in a blind horse, which is often an occasion of the rider's fall.

It was horrid wickedness in Ahab to envy poor Naboth because of his vineyard; and is it a virtue in you that are Christians, to envy others because their outward mercies are greater or sweeter than yours? Has not the Lord given thee himself? Is not one dram of that grace that God has bestowed upon thee more worth than ten thousand worlds? Why, then, shouldst thou envy at others' mercies?

The more the soul is conformed to Christ, the more confident it will be of its interest in Christ.

13*

No pains, no labor, no work like that of the brain, like that of the mind; and none so worthy of praise as those that are most in that labor, in that work. No men's work is so holy and heavenly as a faithful minister's; no men's work is so high and honorable as theirs, and therefore none deserve to be more honored than they, for their works' sake.

Christ has lost none of his affection to poor sinners by going to heaven.

A general doctrine not applied is as a sword without an edge; not in itself, but to the people who, by reason of their own singular senselessness and weakness, are not able to apply it to their own estates and conditions; or as a whole loaf set before children, that will do them no good. A garment fitted for all bodies is fit for nobody; and that which is spoken to all, is taken as spoken to none. Doctrine is but the drawing of the bow; application is the hitting of the mark.

It is not all the talking and profession in the world that can stop the mouths of foolish men;

it must be well-doing, grace improved, grace exercised and manifested in the ways of holiness, that must work so great a wonder; *"For so is the will of God, that with well-doing ye may put to silence the ignorance of foolish men."*

Humility is both a grace and a vessel to receive grace. There are none that see so much need of grace as humble souls; there are none that prize grace like humble souls; there are none that improve grace like humble souls; therefore God singles out the humble soul to fill him to the brim with grace, while the proud are sent empty away.

I could bring in a cloud of witnesses to shame professors in these days, even from among the very heathen who never heard of a crucified Christ, and yet were more crucified to things below Christ than many of them that pretend much to Christ.

A humble soul may groan under afflictions, but he will not grumble in calms. Proud hearts *discourse* of patience, but humble hearts *exercise* patience. Philosophers have much commended it, but in the hour of darkness it is the humble soul that acts it.

What Paul once said concerning bonds and afflictions, that they attended him in every place, the same may believers say concerning temptations, that they attend them in every place, in every calling, in every condition, in every company, in every service; but, that the hearts of his people and temptations may not meet, the Lord is pleased to strengthen them by his best and choicest gifts.

It is dangerous to love to be wise above what is written; to be curious and unsober in your desire of knowledge, and to trust to your own capacities and abilities, to undertake to pry into all secrets, and to be puffed up with a carnal mind. Souls that are thus soaring above the bounds and limits of humility, usually fall into the very worst of errors.

If poverty, with Saul, has killed her thousands, riches, with David, have killed their ten thousands.

It is recorded of Severus that his care was not
to look upon what men said of him, or how they
censured him, but to look what was to be done
by him. "God loves," says Luther, "the run-
ner, not the questioner."

Our sins are debts that none can pay but
Christ. It is not our tears, but his blood; it is
not our sighs, but his sufferings, that can satisfy
for our sins. Christ must pay *all*, or we are
prisoners for ever.

It is the greatest glory of a minister in this
world to be high in spiritual work and humble
in heart. Vain glory is a pleasant thing; it is
the sweet spoiler of spiritual excellencies.

"Buy the truth, and sell it not." Remember
you can never overbuy it, whatsoever you give
for it; you can never sufficiently sell it if you
should have all the world in exchange for it.

Christians, the highway to comfort is to mind
comfort less and duty more.

The spouse's lips are described as being like a

thread of scarlet, talking of nothing but a crucified Christ; and thin like a thread, not swelled
with vain and wicked discourses.

Christian, if you would escape Satan's devices,
then *make present resistance to Satan's first motions*. It is safe to resist, it is dangerous to dis-
pute. Eve disputes, and falls in Paradise; Job
resists, and conquers upon the dunghill.

Ministers should preach *feelingly*, experiment-
ally as well as exemplarily; they must speak
from the heart to the heart; they must feel the
worth, the weight, the sweet of those things
upon their own souls that they give out to others. The highest mystery in divine rhetoric is
to feel what a man speaks, and then speak what
a man feels.

The Lord many times breaks our bones, but
it is in order to the saving of our lives and souls
for ever; he gives us a potion that makes us
heart-sick, but it is in order to the making of us
perfectly well, and to the purging of us from
those ill humors that have made our heads ache,
and God's heart ache, and our souls sick and

heavy to death. Therefore, Christian, under all thy afflictions be silent and thankful.

A man by his arm may do much, but it is mainly by reason of its union and conjunction with the head. It is so between a Christian's graces and Christ. The stream does not more depend upon the fountain, nor the branch upon the root, nor the moon upon the sun, nor the child upon the mother, nor the effect upon the cause, than our graces depend upon the fountain of grace. (Psalm cxxxviii. 3; Philippians, iv. 12, 13.)

Surely they do not truly love Christ who love any thing more than Christ.

The Lord Jesus has as great and as large an interest in the weakest saints as he has in the strongest. He has the interest of a Friend, and the interest of a Father, and the interest of a Head, and the interest of a Husband; and therefore, though saints be weak, yea, though they be very weak, he overlooks their weakness, and keeps a fixed eye upon their graces.

Afflictions˙ are but as a dark entry into our Father's house; they are but as a dirty lane to a royal palace.

When the asp stings a man, it does first tickle him so that it makes him laugh, till the poison, by little and little, goes to the heart, and then it pains him more than ever it delighted him. So does sin. It may please a little at first, but it will pain the soul with a witness at last; yea, if there were the least *real* delight in sin, there could be no perfect hell where men shall most perfectly be tormented with their sin.

There is no man on earth that sees himself such a debtor to God as the humble man; he would count it strange folly to be proud of being *more in debt* than another. "It is true," says he, "I have this and that mercy in possession, and such and such mercies in reversion; but by all I am made more a debtor to God."

Many low and carnal considerations may work men to watch their words, their lives, their actions; as hope of gain, or to please friends, or to get a name in the world, and many other such like reasons. But to watch our thoughts, to weep and lament over them, this must needs be from some noble, spiritual and internal principle, as love to God and a holy care and delight to please him.

Ah, souls, it is not a base low thing, but a God-like thing, though we are wronged by others, yet to be the first in seeking after peace. Such actings will speak out much of God with a man's spirit.

Sinner, remember this—*None ever yet obtained an interest in Christ but unworthy creatures.* Was Paul worthy before he obtained an interest in Christ? And what worthiness was in Zaccheus when Christ called him down from the sycamore tree, and told him that this day salvation was come to his house? Though *you* are unworthy, yet *Christ* is worthy. Though you have no merit, yet God has mercy. Though there is no salvation for you by the *law*, yet there is "*plenteous redemption*" in the *Gospel.*

Grace is given to trade with; it is given to lay out, not lay up.

There is no loss that comes so near to a Christian's heart, as the loss of his Lord; for when God goes, all go—when the King removes, all his train follow; and therefore it is no wonder to see a Christian better bear any loss than the loss of his God, for in losing him he loses all.

The Lord defines faith to be a coming to God in Christ; to be a resting, or staying, or rolling of the soul upon Christ. And it is always safest and sweetest to define as God defines, both vices and graces. This is the only way to settle the soul, and to secure it against all the wiles of men and devils, who labor by false definitions of grace to keep precious souls in a doubting, staggering, and languishing condition; and to make their lives a burden and a misery unto them.

Where one thousand are destroyed by the world's frowns, ten thousand are destroyed by its smiles.

I think that oftentimes men charge that upon the devil which ought to be charged upon their own hearts.

God hath bestowed himself as a portion upon as great sinners as any are that as yet have not God for their portion.

As it is the glory of the stock, when the graffs grow and thrive in it, even so it is the glory of Christ when those who are engrafted into him thrive and grow. The name of Christ, and the honor of Christ, are kept up in the world by souls that are rich in grace. They are the persons who make others think well and speak well of Christ.

The worst of men are in a dead sleep, and the best of men are too often in a sinful slumber, and therefore faithful ministers have need to cry aloud, they have need to be courageous and zealous, to awaken both sinners and saints, that none may go sleeping to hell. Cowardice in a minister is cruelty; if he fears the faces of men, he is a murderer of the souls of men.

Sinner, if thou art but heartily willing to be divorced from that wicked trinity, the world, the flesh and the devil, there is no doubt that God will be thy portion.

Those that have a blemish in their eyes, think the sky to be over cloudy ; and nothing is more common to weak spirits, than to be criticising and contending about others' duties, and to neglect their own.

It is dangerous to be more *notion* than *motion ;* to have faith in the head, and none in the heart; to have an idle and not an active faith. It is not enough for you to have faith, but you must look to the acting of your faith upon Christ as crucified, and upon Christ as glorified. Souls much in this will be very little and low in their own eyes. The great reason why the soul is no more humble, is, because faith is no more active.

Believer, the certainty and sweetness of victory will abundantly recompense you for all the pains you have taken in making resistance against the devil's temptations. The broken horns of Satan shall be trumpets of our triumph, and the cornets of joy.

The greatness of a man's sins does but set off the riches of free grace. Sins are debts, and God can as easily blot out a debt of many thousands, as he can a lesser one; therefore let not the greatest rebel despair, *but believe;* and he shall find, that *where sin hath abounded, there grace shall much more abound.*

Psalm lxxxiv. 11. The *sun* denotes all manner of excellency, provision, and prosperity, and the *shield* represents all manner of protection whatsoever; under the name of *grace* all spiritual good is wrapped up, and under the name of *glory* all eternal good is. wrapped up; under the last clause of the verse, *no good thing will he withhold,* is wrapped up all temporal good; and all put together declare God to be indeed an all-sufficient portion.

There is nothing that makes a man so able to preach Christ to the people, as getting Christ within him.

Bethink thee, Christian, thy mercies outweigh thy wants. God's favors and blessings seldom or never come single; there is a series or course of them, and every former draws on a future. They are also all unmerited, and undeserved; they flow in upon thee from the free love and favor

14*

of God. O then, that, with David, you would summon all the faculties of your soul to praise the Lord, who hath freely filled you, and followed you with the riches of mercy all your days!

Men of the greatest excellencies are the main objects upon which the eye of envy is placed.

The teaching of this and that opinion may please a man's fancy, but it is only the preaching of Christ that changes the heart, that conquers the heart, that turns the heart. Peter, by preaching a crucified Christ, converts three thousand souls at once.

Every believer hath a whole God, wholly, he hath all of God for his portion. God is not a believer's portion in a limited sense, nor in a comparative sense, but in an absolute sense; God himself is theirs, he is wholly theirs, he is only theirs, he is always theirs.

Christians act below their spiritual birth and their holy calling, when they suffer their hearts to be troubled and perplexed for the want of temporal things. Could they read *special love* in such gifts? Would their happiness lie in the enjoyment of them? Nay then, believer, let not the want of those things trouble thee, the enjoyment of which could never make thee happy.

It was a capital crime in Tiberius's days to carry a ring or coin bearing the image of Augustus into any sordid place; and shall not Christians be more mindful and careful, that their graces, which are Christ's image, be noways obscured, but that they be kept always sparkling and shining?

Every man is as the objects are with which he converses. A man may better know what he is by eyeing the objects with which his soul does mostly converse, than by observing his most glorious and pompous services.

As the lowest shrubs are freed from many violent gusts and blasts of wind which shake and rend the tallest cedars; so the humble soul is free from a world of temptations that proud and lofty souls are torn in pieces with.

Self-seekers are self-losers, and self-destroyers.

Absalom and Judas seek themselves, and hang themselves. Saul seeks himself, and kills himself. Haman sought himself, and lost himself That which self-seekers think should be a staff to support them, becomes, by the hand of justice, an iron rod to break them ; that which they would have as springs to refresh them, becomes a gulf utterly to destroy them.

I have read of one, who, when any thing fell out prosperously, would read over the Lamentation of Jeremiah, to keep his heart tender, humbled and low. Prosperity does not contribute more to the puffing up the soul, than adversity does to the bowing down of the soul. This the saints by experience find, and therefore they can kiss and embrace the cross, as others do the world's crown.

It speaks out much of Christ within, to own where Christ owns, and love where Christ loves, and embrace where Christ embraces, and to be one with every one that is practically one with the Lord Jesus.

There is nothing in the world that renders a

man more unlike to a saint and more like to
Satan, than to argue from mercy to sinful liberty, from divine goodness to licentiousness;
this is the devil's logic, and in whomsoever you
find it, you may say of him, "This soul is lost."

Bias, a heathen man, being at sea in a great
storm, and perceiving many wicked men with
him in the ship calling upon the gods, "Oh,"
says he, "forbear prayer; hold your peace. I
would not have the gods take notice that you are
here; they surely would drown us all if they
should." Ah, sirs, could a heathen see so much
danger in the society of wicked men; and can
you see none?

Christians, let your souls dwell upon the vanity of all things here below, till your hearts are
so thoroughly convinced and persuaded of the
vanity of them, as to trample upon them, and
make them a footstool for Christ to get up and
ride in a holy triumph in your hearts.

One of Satan's greatest devices to destroy the
saints is this, *By working them first to be strange,*

*and then to be bitter and jealous, and then to bite
and devour one another.*   Christian, take heed !

Every minister's life should be a commentary
upon Christ's life.

That wisdom which a believer has from Christ,
leads him to center in the wisdom of Christ; and
that love which the soul has from Christ, leads
the soul to center in the love of Christ; and that
righteousness which the soul has from Christ,
leads the soul to rest and center in the righteousness of Christ.   True grace is a beam of Christ,
and where it is, it will naturally lead the soul to
him.

*He that spared not his own Son, but delivered
him up for us all, how shall he not with him also
freely give us all things?* O that Christians would
learn to reason themselves out of their fears, and
out of their distrusts, as the apostle does !   O
that they would no longer rend and rack their
precious souls with fears and cares, but rest satisfied in this, that He who has been so kind to
them in spirituals, will not be wanting to them
in temporals.

When you have overcome one temptation, you must be ready to enter the lists with another. As distrust, in some sense, is the mother of safety, so security is the gate of danger. A man had need to fear this most of all, that he fears not at all.

O Christians, how justly may that father be angry with his child who is unwilling to come home? and how justly may that husband be displeased with the wife who is unwilling to ride to him in a rainy day, or to cross the sea to enjoy his company? But is not this your case? is not this just your case, who have God for your portion, and yet are unwilling to die, that you may come to a full enjoyment of him?

Our safety and security lie not in our weak holding upon Christ, but in Christ's holding us fast in his everlasting arms. This is our glory and our safety, that Christ's *left hand is always under us, and his right hand doth always embrace us.*

Those who are weak in grace dwell more upon their sins than upon the Saviour; more upon

their misery than upon free grace and mercy;
more upon that which may feed their fears than
upon that which may strengthen their faith;
more upon the cross than upon the crown; more
upon those that are against them than upon
those that are for them; and this keeps them
low and weak in spirituals, it causes a leanness in
their souls.

It is a very great stumbling block to many
poor sinners to see men who make a high and
boasting profession of Christ, and yet never exercise and show forth the virtues of Christ. They
profess they know him, and yet, by the non-
exercise of his virtues, they deny him.

God's very service is wages; his ways are
strewed with roses, and paved with joy that is
unspeakable and full of glory and with peace
that passeth understanding.

As the weakest faith, if true, gives the soul a
right to all that internal and eternal worth that
is in Christ, so the weakest faith, if true, gives a
man a real right unto all the external favors and
privileges that come by Christ. (Romans, xiv.

1.) This is the standing rule for all the saints
and churches in the world to go by.

No man can promise himself to be wealthy
till night. One storm at sea, one coal of fire,
one false friend, one unadvised word, one false
witness, may make thee a beggar and a prisoner
all at once.

Doubtless, when the soul cleaves to Christ in
the face of all afflictions and difficulties, this carries with it very great evidence of its interest in
Christ. In temporals, men cleave to persons
and things, as their interest is in them ; and so it
is in spirituals also. Christ can not, Christ will
not throw such into hell that hang about him,
that cleave to him.

" *Every tree that bringeth not forth good fruit is
hewn down and cast into the fire.*" It is not
enough that the tree bears not ill fruit, but it
must bring forth good fruit, or else be destroyed.
So it is not enough that we are not thus and
thus wicked, but we must be gracious and good,
else divine justice will put the ax of divine

15

vengeance to the root of our souls, and cut us off for ever.

Weak Christians are afraid of the shadow of the cross.

If a man have not union with Christ, if he be not implanted into Christ, he can do nothing. The soul, by virtue of its union to Christ, may do much; but such as are separated from Christ can do nothing—at least, as they should. Ah, Christians, if you would but put out yourselves to the utmost, you would find the Lord both ready and willing to assist you, to meet with you, and to do for you above what you are able to ask or think.

One of Satan's devices to keep poor souls in a sad, doubting and questioning condition is causing them to be always poring and musing upon sin; to mind their sins more than their Saviour; yea, so to mind their sins as to forget and to neglect their Saviour. Their eyes are so fixed upon their disease that they can not see the remedy, though it be near; and they do so muse upon their debts that they have neither mind nor heart to think of their surety.

The soul of man is more worth than a thousand worlds. And it is the greatest abasing of it that can be to let it doat upon a little sinning earth, upon a little painted beauty and fading glory, when it is capable of union with Christ, of communion with God, and of enjoying the eternal felicity of heaven.

A little will satisfy nature, less will satisfy grace, but nothing will satisfy a proud man's lusts.

The faith of expectance will in time rise up into a faith of reliance, and the faith of reliance will in time advance itself into a faith of assurance.

When Satan perceives that all those trifling, vain thoughts that he casts into the soul do but vex it into greater earnestness, watchfulness and diligence in holy and heavenly services, he often ceases to interpose such trifles and sinful thoughts, as he ceased to tempt Christ when Christ was peremptory in resisting his temptations.

We trust as we love, and we trust where we love; if you love Christ much, surely you will trust him much.

There is no power below that which raised Christ from the dead and made the world, that can break or turn the heart of a sinner.

Repentance is a flower that grows not in nature's garden.

Those souls who, after they have done all, do not look up so high as Christ, and rest in Christ only, casting their services at his footstool, must lie down in sorrow; their bed is prepared for them in hell. But, sinner, "Is it good dwelling with everlasting burnings and with devouring fire?" If it be, why then rest in your duties still; if otherwise, then see that you center only in Christ.

A humble soul highly prizes the least love token, the least courtesy from Christ; but proud hearts count great mercies small mercies, and small mercies no mercies; yea, pride dóes so unman them that they often call mercy misery.

Woe, woe to that soul that God will not spend a rod upon. This is the saddest stroke of all, when God refuses to strike at all. "Nothing," said one, "seems more unhappy to me than he to whom no adversity has happened."

Know ye not that a little leaven leaveneth the whole lump? Ah, how does the father's sin infect the child, the husband's infect the wife, the master's the servant! The sin that is in one man's heart is able to infect a whole world; it is of such a spreading and poisonous nature.

When sin and suffering have stood in competition, many weak Christians have chosen rather to sin than to suffer, which has opened many a mouth, saddened many a heart and wounded many a conscience. Yet such, by their not suffering, have had to endure more than ever they could have done from the wrath and rage of men. Christian, you must suffer rather than sin.

15*

They are none of the best servants that mind their wages more than their work, and they are none of the best Christians that mind their comforts and their incomes more than that homage and duty which they owe to God.

" *When I awake I am still with thee*" (Psalm cxxxix. 18). What we love most, we most muse upon. That which we much like, we shall much mind. Believer, keep up holy and spiritual affections; for such as your affections are, such will be your thoughts.

Sinners are proud and foolish, and because they have no money, no worthiness to bring, they will not come to the Lord Jesus, though he sweetly invites them. Well, sinners, remember this : it is not so much the sense of your unworthiness, as your pride, that keeps you from a blessed closing with the Saviour.

Augustine, by wandering out of his way, escaped one who lay in wait to mischief him. If afflictions did not put us out of our way, we should many times meet with some sin or other that would mischief our precious souls.

When mercy is despised, then justice takes the throne.

Self-seeking blinds the soul, that it can not see a beauty in Christ nor an excellency in holiness; it distempers the palate that a man can not taste sweetness in the word of God, nor in the ways of God, nor in the society of the people of God; it shuts the hand against all the soul-enriching offers of Christ; it hardens the heart against all the knocks and entreaties of Christ; it makes the soul as an empty vine and as a barren wilderness; in a word, there is nothing that bespeaks a man to be more empty and void of God, Christ and grace than self-seeking.

Though another man can not be saved by thy faith, yet he may be blessed with many blessings upon the account of thy faith. It was the Canaanitish woman's faith that brought a blessing of healing upon her daughter. The centurion's faith healed his servant, who was sick of a palsy. *"From that very hour he was healed"* (Matthew, viii. 5–13).

Of all mercies, pardoning mercy is the most

necessary mercy. Thou mayest go to heaven without honor, and without riches, and without the smiles of creatures, but thou canst never go to heaven without pardoning mercy. A man may be great and graceless, he may be rich and miserable, he may be honorable and damnable, but he can not be a pardoned soul without being a very blessed soul, that entitles him to all blessedness—it puts the royal crown upon his head.

Souls that are torn in pieces with the cares of the world will be always vexed and tormented with vain thoughts in all their approaches to God. Vain thoughts will still be crowding in upon him who lives in a crowd of business.

"*If thou faint in the day of adversity thy strength is small*" (Proverbs, xxiv. 10). Man has no trial of his strength till he is in trouble; faintness then discovers weakness.

Faithful ministers do represent the person of the King of kings and Lord of lords. And though the world crown them with thorns, as it did their Lord and Master before them, yet God will crown them with honor. *They shall shine as the stars in the firmament.* You know embassadors have not preferments while they are abroad; but when they come home to their own country then their princes prefix them and put much honor upon them. So will God deal with his embassadors.

Wicked men are the most needy men in the world—yea, they want those two things that should render their mercies sweet, the blessing of God and content with their condition, and.without which their heaven is but hell on this side hell.

Though men can not bring their means to their minds, yet ought they to bring their minds to their means, and learn content in every state.

A humble soul knows that little sins (if I may so call any) cost Christ his blood, and that they make way for greater, and that little sins, multiplied, become great, as a little sum, multiplied, is great; that they cloud the face of God, wound conscience, grieve the Spirit, rejoice Satan and make work for repentance.

When all else is gone, yet a Christian hath his God to live upon as his portion, and that is enough to make up the want of all other things. As he hath nothing that hath not God for his portion, so he wants nothing that hath God for his portion.

The greatest sins do most and best set off the freeness and the riches of God's grace; there is nothing that makes heaven and earth to ring and sound out his praise so much as the fixing of his love upon those who are most unlovely and uncomely, the bestowing of himself upon those who have given away themselves from him.

The least good that is done by the weakest saint is never despised by Christ. *Behold, we have forsaken all, and followed thee, and what shall we have?* (Matthew, xix. 27.) A great *all* indeed; the disciples left a few old boats, and torn nets, and poor household stuff; yet Christ carries it very sweetly and lovingly to them, and tells them in verse twenty-eight that they should *sit upon twelve thrones, judging the twelve tribes of Israel.* The butler may forget Joseph, and Joseph may forget his father's house, but the Lord will not forget the least good done by the least saint.

To look after holy and heavenly works is the best way to preserve the soul from being deceived and deluded by Satan's devices, or by sudden flashes of joy or comfort; holy works being a more sensible and constant pledge of the precious Spirit, begetting and maintaining in the soul more solid, pure, clear, strong and lasting joy.

No man knows how the *heart* of God stands, by his *hand*. His hand of mercy may be toward a man when his heart is against him, as in the instance of Saul and others. And the hand of God may be set against a man when the heart of God is dearly set upon him, as you may see in Job and Ephraim. Nabal is rich as well as Abraham; Ahithophel wise as well as Solomon, and Doeg is honored by Saul as well as Joseph by Pharaoh. Usually the worst of men have most of these outward things, and the best of men have least of earth, though most of heaven.

Your sins may provoke Christ to frown upon you, they may provoke Christ to chide with you, they may provoke him gently to correct you, but they shall never provoke him to give you a bill of divorce.

Till a man comes to have God for his portion, he never comes to be temptation-proof.

No man knows either love or hatred by outward mercy or misery; for all things come alike to all, to the righteous and to the unrighteous, to the good and to the bad, to the clean and to the unclean. The sun of prosperity shines as well upon the brambles of the wilderness as upon the fruit trees of the orchard; the snow and hail of adversity light upon the best garden as well as upon the wildest waste. Health, wealth, honors, crosses, sicknesses and losses are cast upon good and bad men indifferently.

Though Satan can never rob a Christian of his crown, yet such is his malice that he will therefore tempt, in order to spoil him of his comforts. Such is his enmity to the Father, that the nearer and dearer any child is to him, the more will Satan trouble him and vex him with temptations.

Let us do our duties, and let the Lord do as pleaseth him.

Idleness is hateful in any, but most abominable and intolerable in ministers, and sooner or later none shall pay so dear for it as such; witness the frequent woes that are denounced in Scripture against them.   Where should a soldier die but in the field?   And where should a minister die but in the pulpit?

When a man goes from the sun, yet the sunbeams follow him; so when we go from the Sun of righteousness, yet then the beams of his love and mercy follow us.   Christ first sent to Peter, who had denied him, and the rest who had forsaken him.

Such men as are contented with so much grace as will bring them to glory, and keep hell and their souls asunder, will never be rich in grace, or high in comfort and assurance.   Such souls usually go to heaven in a storm.   Oh, how weather-beaten are they before they can reach the heavenly harbor.

16

It was a weighty saying of one, " The spiritual good of a man consists in this, that a man hath friendship with God, and consequently that he lives for him, to him, with him and in him ; he lives *for* him by consent, *to* him by conversation, *with* him by communion, and *in* him by contentation.

Happiness lies not in those things that a man may enjoy, and yet be miserable for ever. True happiness is too big and too glorious a thing to be found in any thing below that God who is a Christian's chief good.

Satan is as old as the world, and is grown very cunning by experience. When he was but a young serpent, he easily deceived and outwitted our first parents ; but now he is *that old serpent*, as John speaks. Yet, notwithstanding all his plots, devices and stratagems, God's chosen ones shall overcome him *by the blood of the Lamb*.

There is a wonder : God is on high, and yet the higher a man lifts up himself, the farther he is from God ; and the lower a man humbles himself, the nearer he is to God. (Isaiah, lvii. 15.)

As earthly portions carry away worldly hearts from God, so when God once comes to be a man's portion, he carries his heart away from the world, the flesh and the devil. All the world can not keep a man's interest and his heart asunder.

The gifts that Jesus Christ gives widen the heart and enlarge the soul of a believer to take in more of himself. Naturally we are narrow-mouthed heavenward, and wide-mouthed earthward; but the Lord Jesus, by casting his jewels, his pearls, his precious gifts into the soul, doth widen, enlarge, and make it more capacious to entertain himself. Christ, by his gifts, causes all doors to stand open, *that the King of glory may come in.*

Remember, Christians, how many there are in the world, who sit sighing and mourning under the want of those very favors that you enjoy. Why does the living man complain? What, out of the grave, and complain? What, out of hell, and complain? This is a man's sin and God's wonder.

The Persians used to write their kings' names in golden characters; so the Lord writes the names of souls rich in grace in golden letters; their names are always heirs to their lives. *The righteous shall be had in everlasting remembrance.*

As the people prized David above themselves, saying, *Thou art worth ten thousand of us,* so should saints lift up Jesus Christ above themselves, and above every thing below himself. He that lifts not Christ up above all, has no interest in Christ at all. He who sets not Christ above all, is not a disciple of Christ.

A soul weak in grace has as much interest in the Lord as the strongest saint has, though he has not the skill to improve that interest. And is not this a singular comfort and support? Verily, were there no more to bear up a poor weak saint from fainting under all his sins and sorrows, and sufferings, yet this alone might do it.

This is your glory, Christians;—in the presence and sight of all your graces, to see the free grace of Christ, and his infinite, spotless, matchless, and glorious righteousness, to be your only comfort and refuge.   Peter was not well skilled in this lesson, and that was the very reason that he fell foulest when his confidence was highest.

Mercy and grace are sometimes upon the bare knee.   Christ stands knocking at sinners' doors; his hands and heart are full of rich and royal presents; and blessed and enriched for ever are those who open to this King of Glory.

Christian, if you would keep humble, if you would lie low, draw forth your artillery, place your greatest strength against the pride of your soul.   The death of pride will be the resurrection of humility.

Christ has given sin its death-wound by his death and resurrection, so that it can not be long-lived, though it may linger awhile in a saint. As a tree that is cut at the root with a sore gash or two, must die within a year, perhaps a month —nay, it may be within a week, though for a

16*

time it may flourish, and have leaves and fruit—
yet it secretly dies, and will very shortly wither
and perish. So Jesus Christ has given sin such
a mortal blow, that it shall never recover its
strength and power more, and we may truly say
it is dead, it is slain.

Though the scorpion be little, yet will it sting
a lion to death; and so will the least sin, if not
pardoned by the death of Christ.

I have read of one who did not fear what he
did, nor what he suffered, so that he might get
riches; "for," said he, "men do not ask how
good one is, or how gracious one is, but how rich
one is." O sirs, the day is coming, when God
will ask how rich your souls are; not how rich
you are in money, or in jewels, or in land, or in
goods, but how rich you are in grace; which
should provoke your souls to strive, in the face
of all discouragements, to be spiritually rich.

A gracious soul may look through the darkest
cloud, and see his God smiling on him, as by a
rainbow we see the beautiful images of the sun's
light, in the midst of a dark and waterish cloud.

We must look through the anger of his correction to the sweetness of his countenance.

Sin gives Satan a power over us, and an advantage to accuse us, and to lay claim to us, as those that wear his badge.

God takes away a little comfort, that He may make room in the soul for a greater degree of comfort. This, the prophet Isaiah sweetly shows: "*I have seen his ways, and will heal him; I will lead him also, and restore comforts unto him, and to his mourners.*" (Isaiah, lvii. 18.) Bear up sweetly, O precious soul! thy storm shall end in a calm, and thy dark night in a sunshiny day. Thy mourning shall be turned into rejoicing, and the waters of consolation shall be sweeter and higher in thy soul than ever. The mercy is surely thine, but the time of giving it is the Lord's.

The law can not condemn a believer—Christ has fulfilled it for him; divine justice can not condemn him—that Christ has satisfied; his sins can not condemn him—they are pardoned through the blood of Christ; and his own conscience, upon righteous grounds, can not condemn him, because

Christ, who is greater than his conscience, has acquitted him.

It is observable in the court of kings and princes, that children and the ruder sort of people are much taken with pictures and rich shows, and feed their fancies with the sight of rich hangings and fine gay things; whereas, such as are great favorites at court pass by all those as things below them, not worthy of their notice; they have business with the *King;* they have the eye, the ear, the hand, and the heart of the king to take pleasure and delight in. So most men admire the poor low things of the world, and are much taken with them; but a man that hath God for his portion, will pass by all the gay and gallant things of the world, for his business is with his God, and his thoughts, and heart, and affections are all taken up with him.

He who will not improve two talents, shall never have the honor to be trusted with five; but he that improves a little, shall be trusted with much. " *The diligent hand maketh rich.*"

There is nothing that speaks out more the

strength of grace in a man than his standing against *sudden* assaults and invasions that by the devil and the world are made upon him. Many a valiant person dares fight in a battle or a duel who yet would be timorous and fearful if suddenly surprised in a midnight alarm.

For a man to have a great name to live, and yet to have but a little life, is a stroke of strokes. To be high in name, and little in worth is a very sad and sore judgment.

Such is the corruption of our nature, that, propound any divine good to it, it is entertained as fire by water ; but propound any evil, and it is like fire to straw. Did God leave men to act according to their natures, they would be all incarnate devils, and this world a perfect hell.

Let those be thy choicest companions who have made Christ their chief companion.

Weak Christians are overcome with little crosses ; the least cross does not only startle them, but it sinks them, and though they have many comforts for one cross, yet their hearts are so damped and daunted that joy and comfort flies away from them, and they sit down overwhelmed. Certainly this speaks out little of Christ within.

Sin may *rebel*, but it shall never *reign* in any saint.

Believer, rememher this: all the honor that God has from you in this life, is from your living up to that light, knowledge, love, fear and faith that he has given you.

It was a good saying of one, " Wilt thou be great? Begin from below ?" As the roots of the tree descend, so the branches ascend. The lower any man is in this sense, the higher shall that man be raised. The lowest valleys have the blessing of fruitfulness, while the high mountains are barren.

There is no surer way for men to have their gifts and parts blasted and withered as to pride themselves in them and rest upon them; to make light and slight of those who want them, or to engage them against those persons, ways and things that Jesus Christ has set his heart upon.

Carnal weapons have no might or spirit in them toward the making of a conquest upon Satan. We have not to do with a weak, but with a mighty enemy ; and, therefore, we had need look to it that our weapons are mighty, and that they can not be unless they are spiritual.

A true penitent has ever something within him to turn from. He can never get near enough to God, no, not so near him as once he was ; and therefore he is still turning and turning, that he may get near and nearer to him who is his chiefest good and his only happiness.

Nothing will better that man, or move that man who is given up to *spiritual judgments.* Let God smile or frown, stroke or strike, cut or kill, he minds it not, regards it not. He is mad upon his sin, and God is fully set to do justice upon his soul. Such a man's preservation is but a reservation unto a greater condemnation. He has guilt in his bosom and vengeance at his back wherever he goes ; neither ministry or misery, neither miracle nor mercy can mollify his heart; and if this soul be not in hell on this side hell, who is?

Many are miserable by loving hurtful things; but they are more miserable by having them. It is not what men enjoy, but the principle from whence it comes, that makes men happy.

Where grace is improved to a considerable height, it will work a soul to sit down satisfied with the naked enjoyment of God without other things.

The mercy is the waiting man's, but the waiting man must give God leave to time his mercy for him.

The more any man improves his graces, the clearer, the sweeter, fuller and richer is his enjoyment of God here. There is no man in all the world who has such enjoyment of God as that man has who most improves his graces. It is not he who knows most, nor he who hears most, nor yet he who talks most, but he who exercises grace most, that has most communion with God, that has the clearest visions of God, and that has the sweetest discoveries and manifestations of his Lord and Master.

Despair is a sin exceedingly vile and contemptible; it is a word of eternal reproach, dishonor and confusion; it declares the devil a conqueror, and what greater dishonor can be done to Christ than for a soul to proclaim, before all the world, the devil a crowned conqueror?

Pheraulus, a poor man on whom Cyrus bestowed so much that he knew not what to do with his riches, being wearied out with care in keeping them, desired rather to live quietly, though poor, as he had done before, than to possess all those riches with discontent; therefore, he gave away all his wealth, desiring only to enjoy so much as might supply his necessities. Let worldly professors think seriously of this story and blush.

It is good to own and acknowledge a little grace, though it be mingled with very much corruption, as that poor soul did in Mark, ix. 24.

He had but a little faith, and this was mixed with abundance of unbelief; yet he says, *"Lord, I believe, help thou my unbelief."* The least measure of faith will make thee blessed here and happy hereafter.

He will not long be a babe in grace who lives out that little grace he has.

No man's grace or experience rises so high, no man's communion with God and divine enjoyment rises so high, no man's springs of comforts or parts rise so high as theirs do who conscientiously wait upon God in private before they wait upon him in the assembly of his people, and who, when they return from public ordinances, retire into their closets, and look up to heaven for a blessing upon public means.

Christians may doubtless look to their graces as evidences of their part in Christ and salvation, and the clearer and stronger they are, the greater will be their comfort ; but they must not look to them as causes.

Private prayer is a golden key to unlock the

mysteries of the word unto us. The knowledge of many choice and blessed truths are but the returns of private prayer. The word dwells most richly in their hearts who are most in pouring out of their hearts before God in their closets.

Secret sins commonly lie nearest the heart, the fountain from whence they take a quick and continual supply. Secret sins are as near to the original sins as the first droppings are to the spring head.

It was long since determined in the schools that penitents had more reason to be thankful than innocents, sin giving an advantage to mercy, to be doubly free in giving and in pardoning, and so the greater obligation is left upon us to thankfulness.

As the tender dew that falls in the silent night, and makes the herbs and flowers to flourish and grow more abundantly than great showers of rain that fall in the day, so secret prayer will more abundantly cause the sweet herbs of grace and holiness to grow and flourish in the soul than all those more open, public and visible duties of religion, which are too often mingled and mixed with the sun and wind of pride and hypocrisy.

To run from Christ is to run from all life, peace and joy. It is to run from our strength, our shelter, our security, our safety, our crown, our glory. Crabs, that go backward, are reckoned among unclean creatures (Leviticus, xi. 10). The application is easy.

Christ was wonderfully faithful and careful in both parts of his priestly office, namely, satisfaction and intercession ; he was his people's only spokesman. Oh, how earnest, how frequent was he in pouring out prayers, and tears, and sighs, and groans for his people in secret when he was in this world, and now he is in heaven, he is still making intercession for them (Hebrews, vii. 25).

All divine strength and power against sin flows from the soul's union and communion with Christ. It is only faith in Christ that makes a man triumph over sin, Satan, hell and the world.

The assurance of our salvation and pardon of sin primarily arises from the witness of the Spirit of God that we are the children of God; and the Spirit never witnesses this till we are believers, for we are sons by faith in Christ Jesus. Therefore, assurance is not faith, but follows it, as the effect follows the cause.

Believer, if you do not bear with the infirmities of the weak, who shall? who will? This wicked world can not, and will not. The world will make them transgressors for a word, and will watch for their halting; and, therefore, you had need to bear with them so much the more. The world's cruelty should stir up your compassion.

Of all graces, faith is the root grace, and if this die, you will find your graces languish. Your hope, love, fear, patience, humility, joy, can never outlive your faith; they live together and they die together.

Oh, the power of private prayer! it hath a kind of omnipotency in it, it takes God captive, it holds him as a prisoner, it binds the hands of the Almighty, yea, it will ring a mercy, a blessing out of the hand of Heaven itself.

The lives of ministers oftentimes convince more strongly than their words; their tongues may persuade, but their lives command.

A humble soul can rejoice in the grace and gracious actions of others, as well as in its own. But proud souls will be still casting contempt and disgrace upon those excellencies in others that they want in themselves.

The fountain has not the less water for the vessel it fills, nor the sun the less light for that it gives forth to the stars; so the Lord Jesus Christ has never a whit the less for what he gives forth unto his saints.

Chrysostom calls humility the root, mother, nurse, foundation and band of all virtue. Basil calls it the storehouse and treasury of all good. What is the scandal and reproach of religion at this day? Nothing more than the pride of professors.

A humble soul is often looking over the wrongs and injuries that he has done to God, and the sweet and tender carriage of God toward him, notwithstanding those griefs and injuries; and this wins him, and works him to be more willing and ready to bear and forgive wrongs than to revenge them.

Though the joint prayers of the people of God together were often obstructed and hindered in the times of the ten persecutions, yet they were never able to obstruct or hinder private prayer. When men and devils have done their worst, every Christian will be able to maintain his private trade with heaven.

Sotomen reports, that the devout life of a poor captive Christian woman made a king and all his family embrace the faith of Jesus Christ. Good works convince more than miracles themselves.

Christ choosing solitude for private prayer, doth not only hint to us the danger of distraction and deviation of thoughts in prayer, but how necessary it is for us to choose the most convenient places we can for private prayer. Our own fickleness and Satan's restlessness call upon us to get into such places where we may freely pour out our soul into the bosom of God (Mark, i. 35).

A humble heart can not be satisfied with so much grace as will bring it to glory, with so much of heaven as will keep it from dropping into hell; it is still crying out, "Give, Lord, give; give me more of thyself, more of thy Son, more of thy Spirit; give me more light, more life, more love."

He who will not improve two talents, shall never have the honor to be trusted with five; but he who improves a little, shall be trusted with much.

God is never better pleased than when his people importune him in his own words, and urge Him with arguments taken from his own promises.

Certainly, the very soul of prayer lies in the pouring out of a man's soul before the Lord, though it be but in sighs, groans, and tears. One sigh and groan from a broken heart is better pleasing to God than all human eloquence.

The humble soul knows that God out of Christ is incommunicable, that God out of Christ is incomprehensible, that God out of Christ is very terrible, and that God out of Christ is inaccessible; and, therefore, he always brings Christ with him, presents all his requests in his name, and so prevails.

Christ frequently joins praying and preaching together; and those whom Christ hath joined together, let no man presume to put asunder (Luke, xxii. 39, 41, 44, 45).

Suffering times are sealing times. The primitive Christians found them so, and the suffering saints in Mary's days found them so. When the furnace is seven times hotter than ordinary, the Spirit of the Lord comes and seals up a man's pardon in his bosom, his peace with God, and his title to heaven. Blessed Bradford looked upon his sufferings as an evidence to him that he was on the right way to heaven.

Though there is nothing more dangerous, yet there is nothing more ordinary, than for weak saints to make their sense and feeling the judge of their condition. Now, this is dishonorable to God, and very disadvantageous to the soul. Sense is sometimes opposite to reason, but always to faith; we must, therefore, strive to *walk by faith*. (2 Corinthians, v. 7.)

There is oftentimes greatest danger to our bodies in the least diseases that hang upon us, because we are apt to make light of them, and to neglect the timely use of means for removing them, till they are grown so strong that they prove mortal to us. So there is most danger often in the least sins. If the serpent wind in his head, he will draw in his whole body after.

Though none of the people of God have the Spirit in this life in perfection, yet every Christian hath so much of the Spirit as will bring him to Christ, and enable him to reach heaven safely at last.

The more our gifts and graces are exercised, the more they are strengthened and increased. *All acts strengthen habits.*

Luther professeth, "That he profited more in the knowledge of the Scripture by private prayer in a short time, than he did by study in a longer space."

Cæsar in warlike matters, minded more what was to conquer than what was conquered; what was to gain, than what was gained; so does a humble soul mind more what he should be, than what he is; what is to be done, than what is already accomplished.

Temptation is God's school, wherein he gives his people the clearest and sweetest discoveries of his love; a school wherein God teaches his people to be more frequently and fervent in duty; a school wherein God teaches his people to be more tender, meek, and compassionate to other poor, tempted souls than ever; a school wherein God teaches his people to see a greater evil in sin than ever, and a greater emptiness in the creature than ever, and a greater need of

Christ and free grace than ever; a school wherein God will teach his people that all temptations are but his goldsmiths, by which he will try and refine, and make his people more bright and glorious.

Oh, Christians! God loses much, and you lose much, and Satan gains much, by this, that you do not walk lovingly together. It is your sin and shame that you do not pray together, and hear together, and confer together, and mourn together, because that in some far less things you are not agreed together. You will not do many things you may do, because you can not do every thing you should do! Ah! God will whip you into a better temper before he has done with you.

The pious examples of others should be the looking-glasses by which we should dress ourselves. He is the best and wisest Christian, that writes in the fairest Scripture copy, that imitates those Christians that are most eminent in grace, and that have been most exercised in closet prayer, and in the most secret duties of religion.

It is better to have a sore than a seared conscience.

"*We have given thee of thine own*," says David. So, Christian, do thou say, "Lord, the love with which I love thee, is thine own; and the faith by which I hang upon thee, is thine own; and the fear by which I fear before thee, is thine own; and the joy with which I rejoice before thee, is thine own; and the patience with which I wait upon thee, is thine own."

That man is doubtless upon the brink of ruin, whose worldly business eats up all his thoughts of God, of Christ, of heaven, of eternity, and of his soul; who can find time for any thing, but none to meet with God in his closet.

God sees us in secret, therefore, let us seek his face in secret. Though heaven be God's palace, yet it is not his prison.

Promises must be prayed over in private; God loves to be sued upon his own bond, when he and his people are alone.

18

Love covereth all sin. Love's mouth is very large. Love hath two hands, and makes use of both to hide the defects of weak saints. O ye strong ones, Christ casts the mantle of his righteousness over your weakness, and will you not cast the mantle of love over your brother's infirmities?

A man may as truly say, the sea burns, or fire cools, as that free grace and mercy should make a soul truly gracious do wickedly.

God keeps an exact account of every penny that is laid out upon him and his, and that is laid out against him and his; and this in the last day men shall know and feel, though now they wink and will not understand.

The sleeping of vengeance causes the overflowing of sin, and the overflowing of sin causes the awakening of vengeance. Abused mercy will certainly turn into fury.

Remember that God is no curious or critical observer of the plain expressions that fall from his poor children when they are in their closet

duties; 'tis not a flow of words, or studied notions, seraphical expressions, or elegant phrases
in prayer, which take the ear, or delight the
heart of God, or open the gate of glory, or bring
down the best of blessings upon the soul; but
uprightness, holiness, heavenliness, spirituality,
and brokenness of heart—these are the things
that make a conquest upon God, and turn most
to the soul's account.

God's hearing of our prayers doth not depend
upon sanctification, but upon Christ's intercession; not upon what we are in ourselves, but
what we are in the Lord Jesus; both our persons
and our prayers are acceptable in the Beloved
(Ephesians, i. 6).

God makes afflictions to be but inlets to the
soul's more sweet and full enjoyment of his
blessed self.

Our union and conjunction with Christ doth
neither mingle persons nor unite substances, but
it conjoineth our affections, and brings our wills
into a league of amity with Christ.

Be careful that you do not perform closet duties merely to still your consciences; you must perform them out of conscience, but you must not perform them only to quiet conscience.

There is no tongue that can express, or heart that can conceive the horrid sins and miseries that pride hath ushered in among the children of men. All sin will go down with a proud heart. Great sins are no sins with such a soul; he makes nothing of iniquities at which the very heathen would blush.

Christ is the sun, and all the watches of our lives should be set by the dial of his motion.

Certainly no man's calling is a calling away from God or godliness. It never entered into the heart of God that our particular callings should ever drive out our general calling of Christianity. Those men are very ignorant or very profane who think themselves so closely tied up to follow their particular callings six days in the week, that they must not intermeddle with any religious duties during those days. God, who is the Lord of time, has reserved some part of it to himself every day. Though the Jews were commanded to labor six days of the week, yet they were instructed also to offer up the *morning and evening sacrifice daily*.

God esteems men's deeds by their minds, and not their minds by their deeds.

Humility will free a man from perturbation and perplexities. That which will break a proud man's heart, will not so much as break a humble man's sleep.

Secrecy is no small advantage to the serious and lively carrying on of a private duty. Interruptions and disturbances from without, are oftentimes quench-coal to private prayer. The best Christians do but bungle when they meet with interruptions in their private devotions.

An idle life and a holy heart is a contradiction.

Some have stronger corruptions to subdue than others, and more violent temptations to withstand than others, and greater difficulties to

wrestle with than others, and choicer mercies to
implore than others, and higher and harder duties of religion to manage than others, and ac-
cordingly they are more strengthened in the
inner man than others.

He who is active and agile, who works as well
as wishes, who adds endeavors to his desires, will
quickly be a cedar in grace.

Chrysostom compares the mystery of Christ,
in regard of the wicked, to a written book, that
the ignorant can neither read nor spell: he sees
the cover, the leaves and the letters, but he understands not the meaning of what he sees. He
compares the mystery of grace to an indited
epistle, which an unskillful idiot receiving, can
not read; he knoweth it is paper and ink, but
the sense he understands not. So unsanctified
persons, though they are never so learned, and
though they may perceive the bark of the mystery of Christ, yet they understand not the mystery of grace, the inward sense of the Spirit in
the blessed Scriptures. Though the devil be the
greatest scholar in the world, and though he
have more learning than all the men in the

world, yet there are many thousand mysteries and secrets in the gospel of grace, and much that is understood by the disciple, that he knows not really, spiritually, feelingly, efficaciously, powerfully, thoroughly and savingly.

Paul, who learned his divinity among the angels, and had the Holy Ghost for his immedi- ate teacher, tells us plainly, " That he knew but in part;" oh, then, how little a part of that part do *we* know!

Many wicked men take more pains to damn their souls and go to hell than *thou* dost to save thy soul and go to heaven.

Believer, be much in *self-judging*. There are none in the world who so much tremble to think evil of others, to speak evil of others, or to do evil to others, as those who make it their busi- ness to judge themselves. There are none who make such sweet constructions and charitable in- terpretations of men and things as those who are most careful to judge themselves. Ah, were Christians' hearts more taken up in examining and condemning themselves, they would not be so apt to judge and censure others, and to carry it sourly and bitterly toward those who differ from them.

It is but a very short time between grace and glory, between our title to the crown and our wearing the crown, between our right to the heavenly inheritance and our possession of it. The short storm will end in an everlasting calm. "*Sorrow may endure for a night, but joy cometh in the morning.*"

"*Sin lieth at the door.*"   The Hebrew word signifies to lie down, or couch like some beast at the mouth of his cave as if he were asleep, but in reality is wakeful and watching, and ready to fly at all who come near him.   Oh, sirs, beware of sin; it sleeps a dog's sleep, that it may take the sinner at an advantage, and fly the more furiously in his face.

Example is the most powerful rhetoric.   The highest and noblest example should be very quickening and provoking; and Christians have set before them the greatest, the noblest pattern

of humility that was ever heard or read of
(John, xiii. 4).

It was a most sweet and divine saying of Bernard. " O saint, knowest thou not," saith he,
" that thy husband, Christ, is bashful, and will
not be familiar in company ; retire thyself,
therefore, by prayer and meditation into thy
closet, or the fields, and there thou shalt have
Christ's presence."

Tears are a kind of silent prayers, which,
though they say nothing, yet obtain pardon ;
and though they plead not a man's cause, yet
they obtain mercy at the hands of God.   As we
see in that great instance of Peter, who, though
he said nothing that we read of, yet weeping
bitterly, he obtained mercy.

Though our private desires are ever so con-
fused, though our private requests are ever so
broken, and though our private groanings are
ever so much hidden from men, yet God eyes
them, records them, and puts them upon the file
of heaven, and will one day crown them with
glorious answers and returns.

There is much of God in that soul that is, upon a gospel account, more careful and skillful to conceal the vices of weak saints than their virtues. Many in these days do justly incur the censure which that sour philosopher, Diogenes, passed upon grammarians, that they were better acquainted with the evils of Ulysses than with their own.

Conscience is God's spy in the bosom, and as a scribe, a registrar, sits in the closet of our hearts, with pen in hand, and makes a memorandum of all our secret ways and secret crimes, which are above the cognizance of men.

Ah, how do relapses lay men open to the greatest trials and worst temptations! How do they darken and cloud former assurances and evidences for heaven! They give Satan an advantage to triumph over Christ; they make the work of repentance more difficult; they make a man's life a burden, and they render death very terrible to the soul.

It is sad in these knowing times to think how few there are who know the right way of bringing down the power of any sin. Few look so high as a crucified Christ for power against their powerful sins. One soul sits down and complains, "such a lust haunts me; I will pray it down." Another says, "such a sin follows me, I will hear it down, or watch it down, or resolve it down;" and so a crucified Christ is not in all their thoughts. Not but that we are to hear, pray, watch and resolve against our sins; but that, above all, we should look to the acting of faith upon our glorious Redeemer.

There are many that go a round of duties, as mill horses go their round in a mill, and rest upon them when they have done, using the means as mediators, and so fall short of Christ and heaven at once. Open profaneness is the broad road that leads to hell, but closet duties rested in, is a sure though cleaner path.

Whatever faith touches it turns into gold, that is, into our good. If faith looks upon God, it says, *This God is my God for ever and ever, he shall be my guide even unto death.* When it looks upon the crown of righteousness, it says, "This crown is laid up for me." Faith is a sword to defend us, a guide to direct us, a staff to support us, a friend to comfort us, and a golden key to open heaven unto us. Faith, of all graces, is the most useful grace to the soul of man. *Without faith it is impossible to please God.*

No man knows what mercies a day may bring forth, what miseries, what good, or what evil, what afflictions, what temptations, what liberty, what bonds, what good success, or what bad success a day may bring forth; and, therefore, a man need every day be in his closet with God, that he may be prepared and fitted to entertain and improve all the occurrences, successes and emergencies that may attend him in the course of his life.

Much of this world's goods does usually cause great distraction, great vexation, and great condemnation at last to the possessors of them. If God give them in his wrath, and does not sanctify them in his love, they will at last be witnesses against a man, and millstones for ever to sink him in that day when God shall call men to an account, not for the *use*, but for the *abuse of mercy.*

Christian, one smile of Christ, one glimpse of Christ, one good word from Christ, one look of love from Christ in the days of trouble and darkness, will more revive and refresh the soul than all your former service and experiences. Christ is the crown of crowns, the glory of glories and the heaven of heavens.

The spirit is willing, but the flesh is weak. Every new man is two men; he has contrary principles in him, the flesh and the spirit. The spirit, the noble part, is willing; but the flesh, the ignoble part, is weak and wayward.

A soul that is rich in grace says, " Well, ordinances are not *Christ*, refreshings are not *Christ*, meltings are not *Christ*, enlargements are not *Christ*. They are sweet, but he is more sweet; they are very precious, but he is more precious ;" and thus, those who are spiritually rich, do outreach all others.

A weak Christian should be very studious to observe how his heart stands Godward ; for the man is as his heart is; if that be right with Christ, then all is well; therefore says Solomon,

Keep thy heart with all diligence, for out of it are the issues of life.

Repentance is a grace, and must have its daily operations, as well as other graces. A true penitent must go on from faith to faith, from strength to strength; he must never stand still or turn back. True repentance is a continued spring, where the waters of godly sorrow are always flowing. *"My sin is ever before me."*

God expects that we should be his remembrancers, and that we should pray over his promises. Gracious promises are God's bonds, and he loves to see his people put them in suit.

Joy and comfort are those dainties, those sweetmeats of heaven, that God doth not every day feast his people with; every day is not a wedding day, nor is every day a harvest day, nor every day a summer's day.

A humble soul, being once in a great conflict with Satan, said thus to him, "Satan, reason not with me, I am but weak; if thou hast any thing to say, say it to Christ; he is my advocate, my strength and my Redeemer; he shall plead for me." There is no surer way of vanquishing the foul fiend than this.

All tears will not be clean wiped from our eyes till all sin be taken out of our hearts.

Clothe yourselves with the silk of piety, with the satin of sanctity, and with the purple of modesty, and God himself will be a suitor to you. Let not the ornaments upon your backs speak out the vanity of your hearts.

Christian, whenever thou comest off from holy services, sit down and look over the spots, blots and blemishes that cleave to the choicest of them. Thou canst not be proud of them then.

"I have known a good old man," says Bernard, "who, when he heard of any one that had committed some notorious offense, was wont to say within himself, He fell to-day, so may I to-morrow." Now, the reason why humble souls keep up in themselves a holy fear of falling, is because that is the very best way to preserve them in their upward path. "*Happy is the man that feareth always ; but he that hardeneth his heart shall fall into mischief.*"

Cassianus reports that when a certain Christian was held captive by the infidels, and tormented by divers pains and ignominious taunts, being demanded, by way of scorn and reproach, "Tell us what Christ has done for you?" he answered, "He hath done what you see, that I am not moved at all the cruelties and contumelies you cast upon me."

As chickens find warmth by close sitting under the hen's wings, so the graces of the saints are enlivened, cherished and strengthened by the sweet secret influences which their souls fall under when they are in closet communion with their God.

Divine love is like a rod of myrtle, which, as Pliny reports, makes the traveler who carries it in his hand so lively and cheerful that he never faints or grows weary. Ah, friends, did you but love the Lord Jesus with strong love, you would never faint or grow weary of closet duties.

The Lord has often uncrowned himself to crown his people's graces, why, then, should not his people uncrown their graces to crown him? That which others attribute to your graces do you attribute to the God of grace. You must say: Though our graces are precious, yet Christ is more precious; though they are sweet, yet Christ is most sweet; though they are lovely, yet Christ is altogether lovely. Your graces are but Christ's hands by which he works; be you therefore careful that you do not more mind the workman's hands than the workman himself.

The conflict that is in the saints is in the same faculties; there is the judgment against the judgment, the mind against the mind, the will against the will, the affections against the affections; that is, the regenerate part wars against the unregenerate part in all the parts of the soul: but in wicked men, the conflict is not in the same faculties, but between the conscience and the will.

Humility makes a man like an angel, but

19*

pride makes an angel a devil. Pride is worse than the devil, for the devil can not hurt thee till pride hath possessed thee. Proud souls are Satan's apes, none imitate him to the life like these; for as face answers to face in a glass, so does a proud soul answer to Satan.

Fervency feathers the wings of prayers, and makes them fly to heaven. An arrow if it be drawn up but a little way flies not far; but if it be drawn up to the head it will fly far and pierce deeply. So fervent prayer flies as high as heaven and will certainly bring down blessings from thence.

If you can not pray as you would, nor as you should, pray as well as you can.

It was a choice saying of Austin, "Every saint is God's temple, and he who carries his temple about him, may go to prayer when he pleaseth."

Spiritual sluggards are subject to the saddest strokes. Oh, the deadly sins, the deadly temptations, the deadly judgments that spiritual sluggards will unavoidably fall under. None such an enemy to himself, none such a friend to Satan, as the spiritual sluggard.

Laban's house was full of idols; great houses often are so. Jacob's tent was little, but the true worship of God was in it. 'Tis infinitely better to live in Jacob's tent than in Laban's house.

Till we have sinned Satan is a parasite; when we have sinned he is a tyrant.

Private prayer is so far from being an hindrance to a man's business, that it is the way of ways to bring down a blessing from heaven upon it; as the first fruits that God's people gave to him, brought down a blessing upon all the rest. Prayer and provender never hinder a journey.

"Lord," a true believer will say, "do but keep down my sins, and keep up my heart in a way of honoring thee under all my troubles, and then my troubles will be no troubles, my afflictions will be no afflictions. Though my burdens be doubled, and my troubles be multiplied, yet do but help me to honor thee by believing in thee, by waiting on thee, and by submitting to thee, and I shall sing care away; I shall say, it is enough."

Weak Christians are like children; they look for a great reward for a little work. Let their will be but crossed a little by servants, children, friends, or let them but suffer a little in their names or estates, and presently you will hear them sighing out, "No sorrow like my sorrow; no loss like my loss; no cross like my cross;" instead of remembering that an eye fixed upon encouragements, makes heavy afflictions light, long afflictions short, and bitter afflictions sweet.

A Christian should trade with God upon the credit of Christ. "O Lord," he should say, "I need power against such and such sins, give it me upon the credit of Christ's blood. I need strength for such and such services, give it me upon the credit of Christ's word. I need such and such mercies for the cheering, refreshing, quickening, and strengthening of me; give them into my bosom upon the credit of Christ's intercession."

Naturalists report of the Chelidonian stone,

that it will retain its virtue no longer than it is enclosed in gold. So hypocrites will keep up their duties no longer than they are fed and encouraged by the praises of men.

Zeal, ordered by wisdom, feeds upon the *faults* of offenders, not on their *persons*. It spends itself and its greatest heat principally upon those things which concern a man's *self*.

A humble soul can never be good enough; it never can pray enough, or hear enough, or mourn enough, or believe enough, or love enough, or fear enough, or joy enough, or repent enough, or loathe sin enough, or be humble enough.

Weak Christians are usually carried out much after the poor low things of this world. Their hearts should be only in heaven, and yet they strive for earth as if there were no heaven, or as if earth were better; all which does clearly evidence that their graces are very weak, and their corruptions very strong. Men who have little of the "upper springs" within are carried out much after the springs below.

There is no overcoming of God but in his own strength. Jacob did more by his royal faith than he did by his noble hands; more by weeping than he did by wrestling, and more by praying than he did by all his bodily strivings.

Wise men give their choicest and richest gifts in secret; and so doth Christ give his loved ones the best when they are all alone. But as for such as can not spare time to seek God in secret, they sufficiently manifest that they have little friendship or fellowship with Him to whom they so seldom come.

Believer, the more worldly business lies upon thy hand, the more need thou hast to keep close to thy closet. Much business lays a man open to many sins, many snares, and many temptations.

When God hears our prayers, 'tis neither for our own sakes, nor yet for our prayer's sake; but it is for his own sake, and his glory's sake, and his promise sake.

Happy is that soul, and to be equaled with

angels, who is willing to suffer, if it were possible, as great things for Christ as Christ hath suffered for him.

He who casts off private prayer under any pretense whatsoever, casts off the authority and dominion of God, and this may be as much as a man's life and soul are worth.

Believer, you can not have too frequent communion with God, or too frequent intercourse with Jesus. You can not have your heart too frequently filled with joy unspeakable, and full of glory, and with that peace which passes understanding. You can not have heaven too often brought down into your hearts, or your hearts too often carried up to heaven, and therefore you can not be too frequent in closet prayer.

Pride, passion, and other vices, in these days go armed. Touch them never so gently, yet, like the nettle, they will sting you; and if you deal with them roundly, roughly, and cuttingly, they will turn and taunt you, as the Hebrew did to Moses, " Who made thee a judge over us?"

There is wisdom required to present Christ freely to souls, in opposition to all unrighteousness, and to all unworthiness in man. There is wisdom required to suit things to the capacities and conditions of poor souls, to make dark things plain, and hard things easy. Ministers must not be like him in the emblem, who gave straw to the dogs, and a bone to the ass, but they must suit all their discourses to the conditions and capacities of poor creatures, or else all will be lost, time lost, pains lost, God lost, heaven lost, and souls lost for ever.

This age is full of monsters who envy every light that outshines their own, and who throw dirt upon the graces and excellencies of others, that themselves only may be honored.

Prayer is nothing but the breathing *that out* before the Lord, that was first breathed *into us* by the Spirit of the Lord.

The children of God have always cause to exercise faith and hope on him in their darkest condition, though they have not always actual joy and consolation; the Comforter always abides with the saints, though he doth not always comfort them.

As every sacrifice was to be seasoned with salt, so every mercy is to be sanctified by prayer. As gold sometimes is laid, not only on cloth and silk, but also upon silver, so prayer is that golden duty that must be laid, not only upon all our natural and civil actions, as eating, drinking, buying, and selling, but also upon all our silver duties, upon all our most religious and spiritual performances.

God will for ever keep house with the humble soul; when once they meet, they never part. There is no such way to be rich, as to be poor and low in our own eyes. This is the way to enjoy His company in whom all treasures are.

Those years, months, weeks, days, and hours, that are not filled up with God, with Christ, with grace, and with duty, will certainly be filled up with vanity and folly. The neglect of one day, of one duty, of one hour, would undo us, if we had not an Advocate with the Father.

The poorest servant in a family hath a soul more precious than heaven and earth; and the greatest work that lies upon his head in this world, is to look to the eternal safety and security of that treasure, for if that be safe, all is safe, if that be well, all is well, but if that be lost, all is lost.

Weak Christians are apt to sit down troubled and disheartened by the sin within. But they should remember, to strengthen them against all discouragements, that their persons stand before God clothed with the righteousness of their Saviour, and so God owns them, and looks upon them with great delight.

Parents who have but some drops of that love and tender affection which is in God to his people, yet accept of a very little service from their weak children, and will not "Our Father?" In time of strength God looks for much, but in the time of weakness God will bear much, and overlook much, and accept of a little, yea, of a very little. Noah's sacrifice could not be great, yet it was greatly accepted by God. In the time of the law God accepted a handful of meal for a

sacrifice, and a grip of goat's hair for an obla-
tion; and, certainly, he has lost none of his
affection to poor souls since the time of the Gospel.

Cold prayers bespeak a denial, but fervent
supplications offer a sacred violence to the kingdom of heaven. Lazy prayers never procure
noble answers. Lazy beggars may starve for all
their begging.

Some there are who sin away shame, instead
of being ashamed of sin.

The more infirmities and weaknesses that hang
upon us the more cause have we to keep close
and constant to our closet duties. If grace be
weak, the omission of private prayer will make
it weaker. If corruptions are strong, the neglect
of private prayer will make them stronger. The
more the remedy is neglected, the more the disease is strengthened.

Pride is like certain flies, which alight espe-
cially upon the fairest wheat and the loveliest
roses. A proud cardinal, in Luther's time, said,

" A reformation is indeed needful and to be desired, but that Luther, a rascally friar, should be the man to do it, is intolerable."

He that hath no heart to pray for a mercy he needs, hath no ground to believe that God will ever give him that mercy. There is no receiving without asking, no finding without seeking, no opening without knocking.

You had better be a poor man and a rich Christian, than a rich man and a poor Christian. You had better do any thing, bear any thing, and be any thing rather than be a dwarf in grace.

God, saith Calvin, often recompenses the shadows and seeming appearances of virtue, to show the complacency he takes in the ample rewards that he hath reserved for true and sincere piety.

Full vessels will bear many a knock, many a stroke, and yet make no noise; so Christians, who are full of Christ and full of the Spirit, will

bear many a blow, many a stroke without murmuring.

Every Christian has three advocates pleading
for him. The first is that divine love which is
in the bosom of the Father, the second is the
Lord Jesus, who is at the right hand of the
Father, and the third is the Holy Spirit, who is
one with the Father.

Christians, fix yourselves under the ministry
of one who gives the Father his due, the Son
his due, and the Spirit his due; who makes it
his business to open the treasures and the riches
both of the one and the other, and to declare to
you the whole will of God; for many there are
who withhold the word in unrighteousness, and
who will only acquaint you with some parts of
the will of God, keeping you ignorant of the
rest, whose condemnation will be great as well
as just.

Sinful omissions lead to sinful commissions.

'Twas an excellent saying of Ambrose, "If
thou canst not hide thyself from the sun, which

is God's minister of light, how impossible will it be to hide thyself from him whose eyes are ten thousand times brighter than the sun! Though a sinner may baffle his conscience, yet he can not baffle the eye of God's omnisciency.

"Pride," saith Hugo, "was born in heaven, but forgetting by what way she fell therefrom, she could never find her way thither again."

The gospel drops nothing but marrow and fatness, love and sweetness; and therefore God looks in these days that men should grow up to a greater height of holiness, heavenliness and spirituality than what they attained to in those dark days wherein the sun shone but dimly.

A Christian's whole life should be a visible representation of Christ. The heathens had this notion among them, as Lactantius reports, that the way to honor their gods was to be like them. Sure I am that the best way of honoring Christ is to be like him (1 John, ii. 6): "He that saith he abideth in him ought himself also to walk even as he walked." Oh, that this blessed Scripture might always lie warm upon our hearts.

Although Christians do not share in the honors, profits, pleasures and advantages of the world ; yet this should be their joy and crown, that Christ and their souls are sharers in those things that are most eminent and excellent, most precious and glorious ; and the serious remembrance hereof should bear up their heads, hopes and hearts above all the troubles, temptations and afflictions that come upon them in this world.

That Christian, or that minister who, in private prayer, lies most at the feet of Jesus, shall certainly understand most of the mind of Christ in the gospel, and he shall have most of heaven and the things of his own peace brought down into his heart.

No man can make sure or happy work in prayer but he who makes heart work of it. When the soul is separated from the body, the man is dead ; and so when the heart is separated from the lip in prayer, the prayer is dead.

Believer, consider this : *living up to your graces carries with it the greatest evidence of the truth of grace.* That man who lives not up to his grace, let him be strong or weak, wants one of the best and clearest demonstrations that can be to evidence the truth of his grace. If you would be sure that that little love, that little faith, that little zeal you have is true, then live up to that love, live up to that faith, live up to that zeal that you have, and this will be evidence beyond all contradiction.

The heart is the spring and fountain of all natural and spiritual actions; it is the *primum mobile,* the great wheel that sets other wheels going; therefore keep it with all custody and caution, or else bid farewell to all true joy, peace and comfort.

Those shall be sure to fall short of divine acceptance, and of a glorious recompense, who are not able to look above the praises of men.

There is great truth in that old saying, " That duties are esteemed not by their acts, but 'by their ends." As the shining sun puts out the fire, so the glory of God must consume all other ends. Two things make a good Christian—good actions and good aims. And though a good aim doth not make a bad action good, as with Uzzah, yet a bad aim makes a good action bad, as in Jehu's case, whose justice was approved, but his policy punished. God writes "Nothing" on all those services wherein men's ends are not right.

Luther, in his preaching, met with every man's temptation, and being once asked how he could do so, answered, "Mine own manifold temptations and experiences are the cause thereof."

If the prayers of God's children are so faint that they can not reach up as high as heaven, then God will bow the heavens and come down to their prayers.

When Satan prevails over the saints, he says, "Look, O Christ, are these the price of thy blood? Are these the objects of thy love? Are these the delight of thy soul? What, are these thy jewels? Are these the apple of thine eye? Are these thy pleasant portion? Why, lo, how I lead them! Lo, how I triumph over them! They seem rather to be mine than thine." Ah, Christians, resist as for life, that Satan may never have occasion thus to insult and triumph over Christ.

Every mercy that is gathered by the hand of private prayer is as sweet as the rose of Sharon; but those blessings which are received without either supplication or thanksgiving, lack the precious perfume of a Saviour's love, and leave no fragrance in the ungrateful heart.

There is not a sin that a saint commits but Satan would trumpet it out to the world if God would give him leave.

It is sad to consider how few professors in these days have attained the right way of mortifying sin. They usually go out against their sins in the strength of their own purposes, prayers and resolutions; and scarcely look so high as a crucified Christ. They mind not the exercise of their faith upon Christ, and therefore it is a righteous thing with him that they should be carried away captive by their sins. Oh, if men would believe in Christ more, sin would die more.

When the house is on fire, if a man should only pray or cry, he may be burnt for all that; therefore he must be active and stirring; he must run from place to place and call out for help, and bestir himself as for life in the use of all means whereby the fire may be quenched. So grace must be acted on; it is not all a man's praying and crying that will profit him or better him; grace must be exercised, or all will be lost —prayers lost, tears lost, time lost, strength lost, soul lost.

The world gives *a little*, that it may give no more; but Christ gives "that he may give." He gives a little grace, that he may give grace upon grace. He gives a little comfort, that he may give fullness of joy. He gives some sips, that he may give full draughts. He gives pence, that he may give pounds; and he gives pounds, that he may give hundreds.

When God crowns us, he doth but crown his

own gifts in us; and when we give God the glory of all we do, we do but give him that which is due unto his name, for it is he, and he alone, that works all our works in us and for us.

The highest honor and glory that earthly princes can put upon their subjects is to communicate to them their greatest secrets. Now this high honor and glory the King of kings hath put upon his people: "For his secrets are with them that fear him, and he will show them his covenant."

"We, then, that are strong," says the apostle, "ought to bear the infirmities of the weak." Mark, he does not say the enormities, but the infirmities; he does not say the wickedness, but the weakness. The Lord bears with the weakness of his children. Peter is weak, and sinful through weakness; but the Lord Jesus carries it tenderly and lovingly toward him still. Thomas is very weak: "I will not believe," says he, "except I shall see in his hands the print of the nails, and thrust my hand into his side." Now this Christ bears with much patience and sweetness: "Then said he to Thomas, reach hither thy finger, and behold my hands; and reach hither thy hand, and thrust it into my side; and be not faithless, but believing" (John, xx. 27). The Lord Jesus does, as it were, open his wounds afresh; he overlooks his weakness. "Well," says he, "seeing it is so, that thou wilt not believe, I will rather bleed afresh than that thou shouldest die in thy unbelief." Oh, how compassionate is our precious Lord!

Oh, weak and timid Christian, thou shouldst be greatly thankful for the little grace thou hast. Does free grace knock at thy door when it passes by the doors of thousands? Does it cast a pearl of price into thy bosom when others are lying in their blood for ever? And wilt thou not be thankful? Remember, the least measure of grace is worth more than a thousand worlds, yea, worth more than heaven itself!

Much faith will yield unto us *here* our heaven, but *any* faith, if true, will yield us heaven hereafter.

Some of the learned think that Christ intercedes only by virtue of his merits; others, that it is done only by his speech. I think it may be done both ways, because Christ hath a tongue and body glorified in heaven ; and is it likely that that tongue which pleaded so much for us on earth, should be altogether silent on our behalf when in heaven ?

'Tis thy duty to perform closet duties, but it is thy sin to rely on them, or to put confidence in them ; do them thou must, but glory in them thou must not. He who rests in his closet duties, makes a Saviour of them. Let them lead thee to Jesus, and leave thee more in communion with him, and in dependence upon him, and then thrice happy shalt thou be. Let thy closet prayers, tears, and meltings, be a star to guide thee to Jesus, a Jacob's ladder by which thou mayest ascend into the bosom of eternal love, and then thou art safe for ever.

Of all gifts, Christ is the sweetest gift. As the tree in Exodus, xv. 25, " sweetened the bitter waters," so this gift, the Lord Jesus, of whom that tree was a type, sweetens all other gifts that are bestowed upon the sons of men. He turns

every bitter into sweet, and makes every sweet
more sweet.

Many preachers in our days are like Hera-
clitus, who was called the dark doctor. They
affect sublime notions, obscure expressions, and
uncouth phrases, making plain truths difficult,
and easy truths hard. "They darken counsel
with words without knowledge." Studied expressions and high notions in a sermon, are like
Ashael's carcass in the way, that did only stop
men, and make them gaze, but did no ways profit
or edify them. It is better to present truth in
her native plainness than to hang her ears with
counterfeit pearls.

It is more a weakeness than a virtue in strong
Christians, when a weak saint is fallen, to aggra-
vate his fall to the uttermost, and to present his
sins in such a dreadful dress as shall amaze him.
He who shall lay the same strength to the rubbing of an earthen dish, as he does to the rubbing
of a pewter-platter, instead of cleaning it will
surely break it to pieces. The application is
easy.

Absolute perfection is peculiar to the triumphant state of God's elect in heaven; that is the only privileged place where no unclean thing can enter; the only place where sin and Satan and hell never obtained a footing. Such as dream of an absolute perfection in this life confound and jumble heaven and earth together. Absolute perfection is not a step short of heaven, 'tis heaven this side heaven; and they who would obtain it must step to heaven before they have it.

There is no receiving without asking; no finding without seeking; no opening without knocking. The threefold promise annexed to the threefold precept should encourage all Christians to be instant, fervent, and constant in prayer. (Matthew, vii. 7.)

A man's most glorious actions will at last be found to be but glorious sins, if he hath made *himself,* and not the glory of God, the end of those actions.

Grace is compared to the sweetest things, to sweet spices, and to wine and milk. Grace is a beam of that Sun of righteousness, the Lord Jesus Christ. Grace is a sweet flower of Paradise, a spark of glory. It is cherished and maintained by that sweet word, which is sweeter than honey or the honeycomb, and by sweet union and communion with the Father and the Son. It is exercised about the sweetest objects —God, Christ, the promises, and future glory; and it sweetens all our services and duties.

Secret sins are in some respects more dangerous than open sins. The more inward and secret the disease is, the more the man is in danger of losing his life. There are no fevers so dangerous as those that prey upon the spirits and inward parts: so there are no sins so pernicious to the souls of men as those that are most inward and secret. Secret sins often reign in the souls of men most powerfully when they are least apparent.

Jerome tells us of one Didymus, a godly preacher, who was blind, and Alexander a pious man, coming to him, asked him whether he was not sore troubled and afflicted for want of his sight? "Oh, yes," said Didymus, "it is a great grief and trial to me." Then Alexander chid him, saying, " Has God given you the excellency of an angel, and an apostle, and are you troubled for that which rats, mice, and brute beasts have?"

Tears are not always mutes. "Cry aloud, (saith one) not with thy tongue, but with thine eyes; not with thy words, but with thy tears; for such is the prayer which maketh the most forcible entry into the ears of the great God of heaven." Penitent tears are undeniable ambassadors, they never return from the throne of grace without a gracious answer.

If a man be not interested in Christ, he may perish with "Our Father" in his mouth.

When the world frowns most, then generally God smiles most; when the world puts its iron chains upon the saints' legs, then God puts his golden chains about their necks; when the world puts a bitter cup into one hand, then the Lord puts a cup of consolation into the other; when the world cries out "Crucify them, crucify them," then commonly they hear that voice from heaven,

"These are my beloved ones, in whom I am well pleased."

Believer, closet prayer will be found to be but a lifeless, comfortless thing, if you do not enjoy communion with God in it. That should be the very soul of all your closet duties, therefore press after it, as for life; when you go into your closet banish every thing that can hinder your enjoyment of Christ.

True grace makes all new, the inside new, and the outside new; "If any man be in Christ, he is a new creature."

Want of private duties is the great reason why the hearts of many are so dead and dull, so formal and carnal, so barren and unfruitful under public ordinances. Oh, that Christians would seriously lay this to heart! Certainly that man's heart is best in public duties, who is most frequent in private exercises; they make most earnings in public ordinances, who are most conscientiously exercised in closet communings.

Oh, the horrid drudgery that is in the ways

of sin, Satan, and the world. The worst day in
Christ's service is better than the best day, if I
may so speak in sin or Satan's service. Satan
will pay the sinner home at last with the loss of
God, Christ, heaven, and his soul for ever.

God loves that his people should put his bonds,
(his promises) in suit; and he who does so shall
find God near him though friends should leave
him and the world be in arms against him.

Troubled Christian, bear up bravely; for whatever hardships thou meetest with in the ways of
God, shall only reach thy outward man; and
under all these trials thou mayest have as high
and sweet communion with him as if thou hadst
never known what hardships meant.

There is nothing that so clearly and so fully
speaks out the sincerity and spiritual ingenuous-
ness of a Christian as thankfulness does. Thanksgiving is a self-denying grace; it is the making
ourselves a footstool, that God may be lifted up
upon his throne, and ride in a holy triumph over
all. Self-love, flesh and blood, and many low
and carnal considerations may induce men to

pray, and hear, and talk, but thanksgiving is the free-will offering of a child.

It was the saying of an old saint, that he was more afraid of his duties than of his sins; for the one made him proud, the other made him always humble.

The Lord Jesus gives the best gifts to his own people, that he may fence and strengthen them against the worst temptations. There are no men on earth lie so open to temptation as the saints. The best men have always been the most tempted. The more excellent any man is in grace and holiness, the more shall that man be followed with temptations, as you may see in David, who was tempted by Satan to murder the people; and Job, to curse God and die; and Peter, to deny Christ; and Paul, who was sorely buffeted; yea, and Christ himself was most grievously assaulted. But the Lord knows well enough, that Satan has a cruel, envious, and malicious eye upon his beloved ones, and therefore he is pleased, by his precious gifts, to strengthen them against his assaults.

Heart and tongue must go together; word and work, lip and life, prayer and practice must echo to one another, or else thy prayers and thy soul will be lost together.

An early turning to the Lord will prevent many temptations to despair; many temptations to neglect the means openly, to despise the means secretly; many temptations about the being of God, the goodness, faithfulness, truth and justice of God. Temptations to question all that God has said, and all that Christ has suffered, arise many times from men's delaying and putting off God to the last; all which, with many others, are prevented by seeking and serving the Lord in the morning and springtime of youth.

The curse of unsatisfiableness lies upon the creature. Honors can not satisfy the ambitious man, nor riches the covetous man, nor pleasures the voluptuous man. Man can not take off the weariness of one pleasure by another, for after a few evaporated minutes are spent in pleasure, the body presently fails the mind, and the mind the desire, and the desire the satisfaction, and all the man.

The two poles could sooner meet, than the love of Christ and the love of the world.

Sin is the soul's sickness, and nothing prejudices growth more than sickness. Christians, if ever you would be trees, having not only the leaves of honor but the fruits of righteousness, then take heed of sin, abhor it more than hell, and fly from it as from your deadliest enemy.

Ambrose was wont to say, "I am never less alone than when I am all alone; for then I can enjoy the presence of my God most freely, fully, and sweetly, without interruption."

"Take heed of crying, to-morrow, to morrow," says Luther, "for a man lives forty years before he knows himself to be a fool, and by the time he sees his folly, his life is finished; so men die before they begin to live."

It was a notable saying of Luther, "The church converteth the whole world by blood and prayer." Divers have been won to Christ by beholding the gracious carriage of Christians under reproaches for their Master's sake. Reproach is a royal diadem, it is Christ's livery; therefore, Christian, count it your highest ambition in the world to wear this livery for *his* sake, who once wore a crown of thorns for your sake.

It is a great folly, it is double iniquity, for a Christian to be troubled for the want of those things which God ordinarily bestows upon the worst of men. Oh, the mercies that a Christian has in hand, in hope, and in the promises, are so many, so precious, and so glorious, that they should bear up his head and heart from fainting and sinking under all outward wants.

Closet duty speaks out most sincerity. He prays with a witness who prays without a witness.

Believer, be not impatient or forward when God shall take away some lesser mercies from you. He has given you the best and greatest gifts that your souls can beg, or himself will give, and will you be sighing and mourning when he shall come to take away some lesser favor? Verily, this is the way to provoke God to strip thee naked of thy choicest ornaments, and to put thee in chains, or else to turn thee grazing among the beasts of the fields, as he did Nebuchadnezzar.

It is the greatest measure of grace that ushers in the greatest measure of joy and comfort into a believing heart.

"Lust having conceived, it bringeth forth sin." Sin hath its conception, and that is delight; and then its formation, and that is design; and then its birth, and that is action; and then its growth, and that is custom; and then its end, and that is damnation.

It were ten thousand times better that we had never been born into the world than that we should go unrenewed out of the world.

It was a saying of Bede, " that he who comes not willingly to church, shall one day go unwillingly to hell."

All who grow rich in grace, grow rich gradually. The sun ascends by degrees; children, plants and trees grow by degrees; so do saints in spiritual things. As to temporals, it is true that by the death of a friend, or this and that providence, men may become rich on a sudden; but no soul that is rich in grace attains this treasure suddenly. "The path of the just is as the shining light, which shineth more and more unto the perfect day."

God hears no more than the heart speaks; and if the heart be dumb, God will certainly be deaf.

God, who hath done singular things for our good, may indeed justly expect that we should do singular things for his glory.

We read in Plutarch of a young maid exposed for sale in the market, who, when a chapman asked her, "Wilt thou be faithful if I buy thee?" answered, "Aye, that I will, though you do not buy me." So also must we be found faithful, even though we meet with no encouragement in the work which our Father has given us to do.

Experience in religion is beyond notions and

expressions. A sanctified heart is better than a silver tongue.

A young man, very much given up to pleasures, standing by St. Ambrose and seeing his excellent death, turned to other young men by him, and said, " Oh! that I might live with you and die with him!"

The gifts of the world are fading; a false oath, a spark of fire, a storm at sea, a treacherous friend brings all to nothing in a moment. But the gifts that Christ gives are permanent and lasting. The grace he gives is called an *immortal seed;* and the glory he gives is called *everlasting glory.*

What though, O precious soul, thy language be clipped and broken? What though thou canst not talk so fluently and so eloquently for Christ as others? What though thy hand be so weak that thou canst not do so much for Christ as others, nor do so well for Christ as others? Yet the Lord, seeing thy *heart sincere,* will reward thee. Thou shalt have an everlasting rest for a little labor, and a great reward for a little work.

A *little* of this world's goods will serve a man who is strong in grace; *much* will not serve a man who is weak in grace; *nothing* will serve a man who is void of grace.

"*Behold, I stand at the door and knock; if any man hear my voice and open the door,* let him be never so guilty, never so filthy, never so unworthy, *I will come in and sup with him, and he with me.*" Lord, at whose door dost thou stand knocking? Is it at the rich man's door, or at the righteous man's door, or at the qualified and prepared man's door? "No," says Christ, "it is at none of these doors." At whose then, O blessed Lord? At the lukewarm Laodicean's door; at their door who are neither hot nor cold, who are wretched, and miserable, and poor, and blind and naked? "These," 'says Christ, "are the worst of the worst, yet if any of them shall open the door, *I will come in and sup with him, and he with me.*" Ah, poor souls, Christ is willing to bestow the best gifts upon the worst sinners.

If *any* prayer be a duty, then *secret* prayer

must be superlatively so, for it prepares and fits the soul for all other supplication.

If a tree do not bud, blossom and bring forth fruit in the spring, it generally is dead all the year after; so if in the spring and morning of your days you do not bring forth fruit to God, it is a hundred to one that you bring forth fruit to him when the evil days of old age shall overtake you, wherein you shall say you have no pleasure; for, as the son of Sirach observes, "If thou hast gathered nothing in thy youth, what canst thou find in thine old age?"

Cold prayers are like arrows without heads, swords without edges, birds without wings; they pierce not, they cut not, they fly not up to heaven. Those prayers that have no heavenly fire in them always freeze before they reach as high as heaven; but fervent prayer is very prevalent with God.

Many take unfit seasons for private prayer, which more obstruct the importunity of the soul in prayer than do all the suggestions and importunities of Satan.

22*

Rashness will admit of nought for reason, but what unreasonable self shall dictate for reason.

As sloth seldom brings actions to a good birth, so rashness makes them always abortive ere well formed.

"*Continuing instant in prayer.*" The Greek is a metaphor taken from hunting dogs that never give over the game till they have got their prey. A Christian must not only pray, but hold on in prayer, till he has obtained the heavenly prize. We are daily in want, and therefore we had need be daily praying

Ah, how many threadbare souls are to be found under silken cloaks and gowns! How often are worldly riches like executioners! they hide men's faces with a covering that they may not see their own end, and then they hang them. Yes, and if they do not hang you, they will shortly leave you, for they "make themselves wings and flee away."

By nature we are as full of hard thoughts of God as hell is full of sin; and where the heart is not mightily overawed by the Spirit of God, and overpowered by the grace of God, there all manner of dark and dismal apprehensions of him abound; for Satan knows very well that our corrupt natures are made up of sad and evil thoughts of God, and therefore he uses all his power and craft to stir us up to sin against him. That Christian is a very great stranger to his own heart who is not able to say from experience, that it is one of the highest and hardest works in this world to keep up good and gracious thoughts of God in a suffering condition, or under dark and dismal dispensations.

When we consider that sin has slain our Lord Jesus Christ, O how should the thought provoke our hearts to be revenged on sin, for having murdered the Lord of glory, and done more mischief than all the devils in hell could have done.

All the riches of Christ are unsearchable riches. A saint, with all the light that he has from the Spirit of Christ, is not able to search to the bottom of these treasures; nay, suppose that all the perfections of angels and saints in a glorified estate should meet in one noble breast, yet all those perfections could not enable that glorious creature to fathom the depths of Christ's unsearchable riches. And when believers come to heaven, when they shall see God face to face, shall know as they are known, and shall be filled with the fullness of God, even then they will sweetly sing this song: Oh, the height, the depth, the length, the breadth of the unsearchable riches of our Lord Jesus Christ!

He who will attend closet prayer without distraction or disturbance, must not slip out of the world into his closet, but he must first slip into his closet before he be compassed about with a crowd of worldly employments.

A good name is always better than a great name, and a name in heaven is infinitely better than a thousand names on earth ; and the way to both of these is to be much with God in secret.

As we are never out of the reach of God's hand, so we are never out of the view of God's eye. When we are in the darkest place God hath windows in our breasts, and observes all the secret actings of our inner man. "Can any hide himself in secret places that I shall not see him, saith the Lord?" (Proverbs, xv. 3.)

God loves to see a poor Christian shut his closet door, and then open his bosom and pour out his soul before him.

Hatred stirreth up strife, but love covereth all sins. Love's mantle is very large. Tale-bearers and tale-hearers are alike abominable. Heaven is too holy a place for them.

When grace is improved and exercised, gracious services are easily performed. The more our natural strength is exercised and improved, with the more ease and pleasure are all physical duties discharged; so, the more grace is acted and exercised, with the more profit and delight all Christian services are performed. Such souls find wages in their very work; they find that not only *for* keeping, but also *in keeping of his commandments there is great reward.*

Satan labors might and main to keep your

graces low and poor. You never hurt him less, you never honor Christ less, you never mind your work less than when grace is weak and low. This he knows, and therefore he labors to keep your graces down.

A man never begins to fall in love with Christ till he begins to fall out with his sins. Till sin and the soul be two, Christ and the soul can not be one.

"Work out your own salvation with fear and trembling" (Philippians, ii. 12). The reason why many men's hearts tremble and are so full of fears and doubts, is because they do not make thorough work in their souls; they do not put the question home, whether they have grace or not, an interest in Christ or not. They do not rise with all their strength against sin, nor with all their power to serve the Lord, and therefore fears and doubts always compass them round about.

The conversion of the thief upon the cross is an example without a promise. It is an *example* of late repentance, but where is there a *promise* to late repentance? O sinner, remember it is not examples, but promises, that are foundations for faith to rest on. For, consider, as one of the dying malefactors was saved to teach sinners not to despair, so the other was damned to teach them not to presume. Oh, think seriously of this, and the Lord make you wise for eternity.

Satan watches the Christian's motions, so that he can not turn into his closet, or creep into any place to converse privately with his God, but he follows hard at his heels, and will be continually injecting *into* the soul, or else objecting one thing or another *against* the soul. A Christian is as well able to tell the stars of heaven, and to number up the sands of the sea, as he is able to reckon the many devices that Satan uses to obstruct the soul's private addresses to God.

Faith is one of those glorious ingredients which must make every sermon and every truth work for the soul's advantage. Nothing will conduce to a believer's good and gain, if his graces be asleep.

Self is the only oil that makes the chariot

wheels of the hypocrite move in religious con-
cerns. They are like blazing stars, which, so long
as they are fed with vapors, shine as fixed stars;
but let the vapors dry up, and soon they vanish
and disappear.

Is not the soul more than raiment, more than
friends, more than life, yea, more than all? Then
why do you not labor to enrich your soul?
'Twere better to have a rich soul under a threadbare coat, than a threadbare soul under a golden
garment. If he be a monster among men, who
makes liberal provisions for his servant or his
slave, and starves his wife, what a monster is he
who makes much provision for his baser part,
but none for his nobler nature! Ah, friends, a
slothful heart in the things of God is a very
heavy judgment.

Company and allurements to sin will be found
no sufficient excuse for sin. If Eve lay her fault
on the serpent, and Adam lay his upon Eve,
God will take it off, and lay a curse on both. It
is in vain for the bird to complain that it saw
the corn, but not the pitfall. The God of spirits
and of all flesh will not be put off with any ex-

cuses or pretenses when he shall try and judge the children of men.

As there is no mercy too great for God to give, so there is no mercy too little for us to crave. Certainly that man hath little worth to him, who thinks any mercy not worth a seeking.

As long as there is fuel in the heart for a temptation, we can not be secure. He that has gunpowder about him, had need keep far enough off from sparks; he that is either tender of his credit abroad, or comfort at home, had need shun the very shadow of sin; and he that would neither wound conscience or credit, God or the gospel, had need hate the garments spotted with the flesh.

God lades the wings of private prayer with the sweetest, choicest, and chiefest blessings. Ah! how often hath God kissed the poor Christian at the beginning of private prayer, spoken peace to him in the midst of his prayer, and filled him with light, joy, and assurance upon its close!

Secret duties shall have open rewards. "Thy

23

father which seeth in secret shall reward thee openly." Ah, Christians, did you really believe and seriously dwell on this, you would walk more thankfully, more cheerfully, suffer more patiently, fight against the world, the flesh, and the devil more courageously, lay out yourselves for God, his interest and glory, more freely, live upon what Providence hath given you for your portion more quietly and contentedly, and certainly you would be in private prayer more frequently and abundantly.

There is no other name, no other nature, no other blood, no other merits, no other persons to be justified and saved by, but Jesus Christ. All the tears in the world can not wipe off one sin, nor can all the grace and holiness that is in angels and men purchase the pardon of the least transgression. All remission is only by the blood of Jesus Christ.

Consider the worth and excellency of souls. A soul is a spiritual, immortal substance; it is capable of the knowledge of God, of union with God, of communion with God, and of a blessed and happy fruition of God. Christ left his

Father's bosom for the good of souls ; he assumed man's nature for the salvation of men's souls; Christ prayed for souls, he wept for souls, he bled for souls, he hung on the cross for souls, he trod the wine-press of the Father's wrath for souls, he died for souls, he rose again from death for souls, he ascended for souls, he intercedes for souls, and all the glorious preparations he has been making in heaven these sixteen hundred years are for souls.

Remember, that the good works which Jesus Christ will reward at last are supernatural works; they are the works of God, wrought from God, for God, in God, according to God. They are works that flow from supernatural principles, and they are directed to supernatural ends, and performed in a supernatural way. Now, the sooner a man begins to be good, the more he will abound in these good works, and, doubtless, the greater reward shall he have in heaven. But it must not be forgotten that the best works of hypocrites, and all men out of Christ, are but fair and shining sins, beautiful abominations.

Natural and moral endowments will enable

men to do much, but grace will teach them to do ten thousand times more. There is no work too high or too hard for souls rich in grace; they are choice instruments in the Lord's hands, to do him service, and bring down blessings upon all around them.

Chilo, one of the seven sages, being asked what was the hardest thing in the world to be done, answered, "To use and employ time well."

Ah, young men and women, remember death is oftentimes sudden in his approaches, and you had need therefore to be prepared to meet him. Nothing more sure than death. Nothing more uncertain than life; therefore, turn from your sins, lay hold on the Lord, and make peace with him, so that you may never have to say, as Cæsar Borgia said when he was sick unto death, "When I lived, I provided for every thing but death; now I must die, and am unprepared!"

Youth is the age of folly, of vain hopes, and overgrown confidence. How wise many might have been had they not been wise in their own opinion too early! Lean not to great parts, lean not to natural or acquired accomplishments, lest you lose them and yourselves too. It was an excellent saying of St. Austin, "He who stands upon his own strength shall never stand." Ah, young men, if you must needs be leaning, lean upon precious promises, lean upon the rock that is higher than yourselves, lean upon the Lord Jesus Christ, as John did, who was the youngest of all the disciples. John leaned much, and Christ loved him much. Oh! lean upon Christ's wisdom for direction, upon his righteousness for justification, upon his blood for remission, and upon his all-sufficient merits for salvation.

As a body without a soul, much wood without fire, or a bullet in a gun without powder, so are words in prayer without the spirit of prayer.

There is no way under heaven to be interested in Christ, but by believing. HE THAT BELIEV-ETH SHALL BE SAVED, let his sins be ever so great; and HE THAT BELIEVETH NOT SHALL BE DAMNED, let his sins be ever so little.

THE END.